KB261171

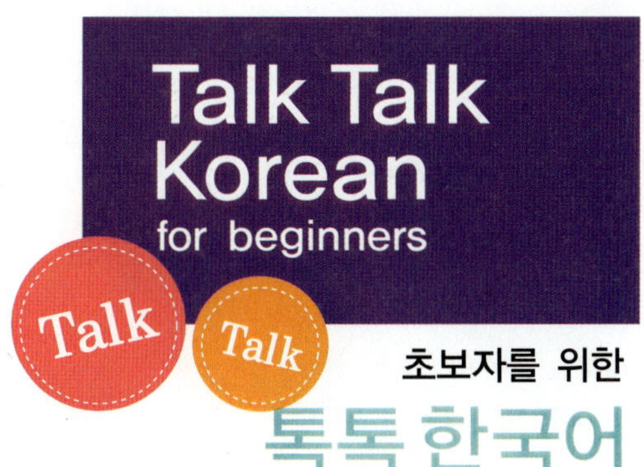
Talk Talk
Korean
for beginners
Talk
Talk
초보자를 위한
톡톡 한국어

## 민진영 Ms. Jinyoung Min

연세대학교 외국어로서의 한국어교육 석사
연세대학교 한국학과 박사 과정 수료
前 경희대, 안동대, 김포대 한국어 강사
現 건국대학교 언어교육원 강사

〈저서〉
『한국어 2(공저)』, 2005, 건국대학교 출판부
『Business 한국어 중급(공저)』, 2007, 재단법인 율촌재단
『2000 Essential KOREAN WORDS for beginners(공저)』, 2008, 다락원
『한국어 5(공저)』, 2009, 건국대학교 출판부

Master of Arts in Education, Specialization in Korean Language Education as a Foreign Language
– Graduate School of Education, Yonsei University.
Ph.D. Candidate in Korean Studies, Graduate School, Yonsei University
Former Korean Language lecturer at Kyunghee University, Andong National University, and Kimpo College
Current Korean Language instructor at Konkuk University

<Published Works>
"Korean 2 (joint project)", 2005, Konkuk Press
"Business Korean Intermediate (joint project)", 2007, The Yulchon Foundation
"2000 Essential KOREAN WORDS for Beginners (joint project)", 2008, DARAKWON
"Korean 5 (joint project)", 2009, Konkuk Press


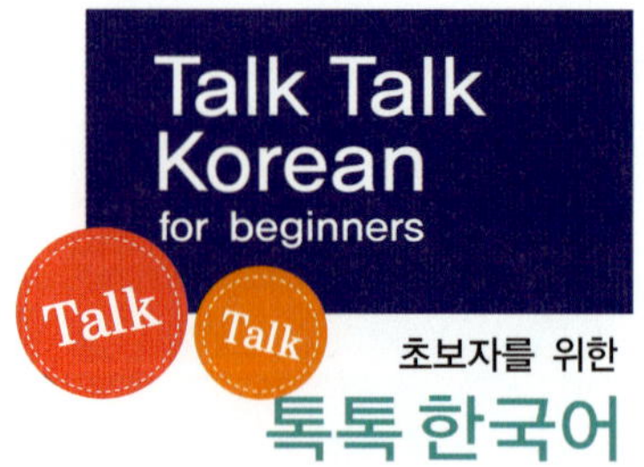



초판 인쇄 2011년 1월 03일
초판 발행 2011년 1월 13일

지 은 이 민진영
펴 낸 이 박찬익
책임편집 최민영
영어번역 Jae Kim
일러스트 김미경

펴 낸 곳 도서출판 박이정
주 소 서울시 동대문구 용두동 129-162
전 화 02)922-1192~3
전 송 02)928-4683
홈페이지 www.pjbook.com
이 메 일 pijbook@naver.com
온 라 인 국민 729-21-0137-159
등 록 1991년 3월 12일 제1-1182호

ISBN 978-89-6292-140-3(13710)

* 책값은 뒤표지에 있습니다.

# Talk Talk Korean for beginners

Talk Talk

민진영

## 초보자를 위한 톡톡 한국어

## 책을 펴내면서

한국어를 가르치면서 많은 외국인들을 만났는데 그들 중에는 한국에서 짧게는 몇 개월, 길게는 몇 년을 살았으면서도 의외로 한국어를 말할 기회가 없었다고 하는 사람들이 있었습니다. 또한 한국어를 배우고 싶어도 시간이 없다는 사람이 많았습니다. 그리고 그들 중에는 굳이 체계적으로 한국어를 배우지 않더라도 한글을 읽고 쓰는 것, 생활에서 꼭 필요한 표현만이라도 배우고 싶다고 말하는 이들이 많았습니다. 그러나 이런 외국인들에게 현재 나와 있는 교재들은 분량도 많고 내용도 많아서 추천하기에는 적합하지가 않았습니다. 그래서 고민 끝에 이 책을 쓰게 되었습니다.

이 책은 외국인들이 한글을 익혀서 읽고 쓸 수 있는 능력과 기초적인 의사소통 능력을 길러 주는 데에 초점이 맞춰져 있습니다. 그래서 이 책은 한국어의 기본이 되는 한글과 일상생활을 위한 서바이벌 한국어로 구성되어 있습니다. '한글 부분' 에서는 단어를 듣고 정확하게 발음을 해 보는 것과 한글의 철자를 정확하게 읽고 쓰도록 하는 데에 중점을 두었고, '서바이벌 한국어' 부분에서는 대화를 통해 간단한 표현을 익힌 후 그것을 외워서 활용하는 데 초점을 두었습니다. 아울러 다양한 그림 자료와 번역을 통하여 한국어를 좀 더 쉽고 재미있게 배울 수 있게 하였습니다.

이 책의 구성내용을 구체적으로 살펴보면 다음과 같습니다. 1장에서는 한글의 창제원리를 비롯해 한글의 전반적인 것을 소개하였습니다. 2장에서는 기본모음과 자음, 복합모음과 받침을 익히도록 하기 위해 먼저 모음과 자음을 제시한 후 단어를 그림과 함께 보여 주어 듣고, 읽고 쓰는 순서를 갖게 하였습니다. 그리고 다양한 활동을 통하여 재미있고 자연스럽게 한글의 기초를 익히도록 하였습니다. 3장에서는 2장에서 익힌 것을 기초로 한국 생활에 기본이 되는 인사말과 자기소개, 쇼핑하기, 택시 이용하기와 같은 표현들을 익히도록 하였습니다. 부록에는 학습에 필요한 단어와 표현 목록을 한국어와 영어로 쉽게 찾을 수 있도록 하였고, 단어와 표현이 들어 있는 그림카드를 제시해 그것을 잘라서 휴대할 수 있도록 하였습니다.

부족하나마 이 책이 한국 생활을 유익하고 재미있게 하고자 하는 외국인들과 한국 사람과 의사소통을 하고 싶어하는 외국인들에게 도움이 되기를 바랍니다.

이 책이 나오기까지는 많은 사람의 노력과 협조가 있었습니다. 기획 단계부터 많은 조언을 해 주신 박이정의 박찬익 사장님과 항상 웃으며 최선을 다해 준 디자이너 최민영 씨에게 진심으로 감사드립니다. 그리고 꼼꼼하게 번역을 해 준 Jae Kim 선생님과 집필 과정을 사랑으로 지켜봐 주고 응원해 준 가족들, 책을 쓰도록 동기를 부여해 준 이해경 선생님, 한국어를 가르치는 교사의 입장에서 같이 고민해 주고 교정을 봐 준 안진명, 이희정, 신현미 선생님을 비롯해 곁에서 힘이 되어 준 동료들과 친구들에게 고마운 마음을 전합니다.

2011년 1월
민진영

# About the Book

As a Korean Language educator, I have met many foreign visitors in Korea. Also, I have met foreigners who have resided in Korea anywhere between a few months and a few years, and many of them stated they have never had the chance to practice speaking Korean. Also I met foreigners who expressed interest in learning Korean, but simply did not have time to study. Also, some foreigners stated that although they had no plans to try to become fluent in Korean, they still wanted to learn basic survival Korean words, reading skills, writing skills, and common expressions for daily use. However, the same foreigners complained that the current Korean language study materials out there either contain too much information, or were too long and drawn out; so they were unsuitable for practical use. After reflecting upon these issues, I decided to write this book.

This book focuses on helping foreigners learn basic Hangeul reading, writing, and conversation skills. Also, this book teaches how to apply Hangeul words and expressions in daily life. The initial 'Hangeul Section' focuses on vocabulary, accurate pronunciation, reading, and how to correctly write Korean handwriting. The latter 'Survival Korean Section' focuses on learning Korean expressions that are used in everyday practical situations. Also, various picture and translation contents are included to make learning the Korean language easier and more fun.

The structural contents of this book are organized as follows. Chapter One introduces the origin and fundamental information about Hangeul. Chapter 2 helps the reader to get familiar with basic Hangeul vowels, consonants, combined vowels, and final consonants; to facilitate this process, this chapter begins by introducing all fundamental Hangeul vowel and consonant letters. Then, the latter part of the chapter teaches vocabulary words through pictures; then it moves on to listening, reading, and writing skills in sequence. On a side note, the entire book includes various activities that help to make the process of learning Hangeul feel more natural, rather than rigid and structured. Chapter 3 involves using the contents learned in Chapter 2 as the basis to learn and become familiar with basic Korean greetings, introductions, shopping, riding taxis, and other expressions used in common situations. The Appendix section contains several lists of essential Hangeul words and expressions that the reader can use for reference; and the contents are organized alphabetically in Hangeul, along with their English definitions for the reader to easily find contents. There are also contents presented in forms of picture cards that contain Hangeul words and expressions; these cards are portable and can be carried around for immediate use.

Although this book may be very general in nature, it is my sincere hope that this book will be practically useful for foreigners who wish to enjoy their life in Korea, and also those who hope to regularly communicate and get to know the Korean people.

The creation of this book was made possible due to the cooperation and hard work of many individuals. I would like to extend my sincerest gratitude to Director Park Chan Il, who provided me with valuable advices from the onset of the planning phase this book, and to the editor-in-chief of this book, Ms. Choi Min Young, for her words of encouragement and personal effort. Also, I would like to offer my most heartfelt gratitude to Mr. Jae Kim for his dedicated and detailed translation work, to my loving family for their continuous support, to Ms. Haekyung Lee for her words of encouragement and support to create this book, to my dear fellow Korean teachers, Ms. Ahn Jin Myung, Lee Hee Jeong, and Shin Hyeon Mi, and to many other colleagues and friends who continue to grant me their love and support to this day.

January 2011
Jinyoung Min

# 차례 contents

## Unit III 서바이벌 한국어 Survival Korean



## Unit IV 부록 Appendix

# 한글소개 Introduction to Hangeul

Chapter 1 한글 The Origin of Hangeul

Chapter 2 모음 Vowels

Chapter 3 자음 Consonants

# Chapter 1 한글 The Origin of Hangeul

Hangeul is the writing system of the Korean language, and it was created by King Sejong, the Fourth King of the Joseon Dynasty, and his Chiphyonjon (translated 'Hall of Worthies') scholars, in 1443 AD. The vowel letters were created by first taking into account the model images of the heavens( · ), earth(—), and humans( ㅣ ), and then combining these elements together in various combinations to create individual letters. The consonant letters were created by modeling after the basic shapes of vocal organs that were created by each consonant sounds.

Hangeul consists of 40 letters, which in turn consists of 21 vowels and 19 consonants. The vowels and consonants are combined with each other to create syllables.

King Sejong took into account the formation of the tongue and mouth when he created the consonant letters; and took into account the formation of the throat and the flow of air through the air passage to create vowel letters. Therefore, Hangeul can be considered the most phonetically accurate written language out of all the languages around the world.

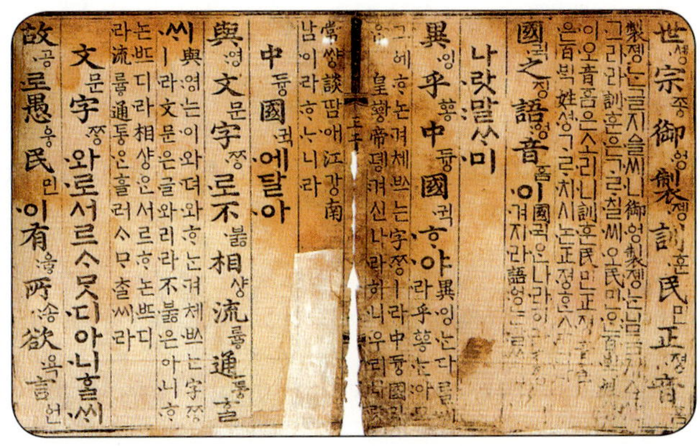

世宗御製訓民正音
國之語音이
나랏말ᄊᆞ미
異乎中國ᄒᆞ야
中國에달아
與文字로不相流通ᄒᆞᆯᄊᆡ
文字와로서르ᄉᆞᄆᆞᆺ디아니ᄒᆞᆯᄊᆡ
故로愚民이有所欲言

훈민정음 해례본 (Hunminjeongeum Haeryebon)

세종대왕 (King Sejong)

# Chapter 2 모음 Vowels

There are a total of 21 vowels in Hangeul. These are divided into 10 basic vowels and 11 combined vowels, which are formed by combining several basic vowels.

## 1) 모음의 구성 원리 Fundamental Characteristics of Hangeul Vowels

The basic shapes of the vowels were modeled after the following three elements.

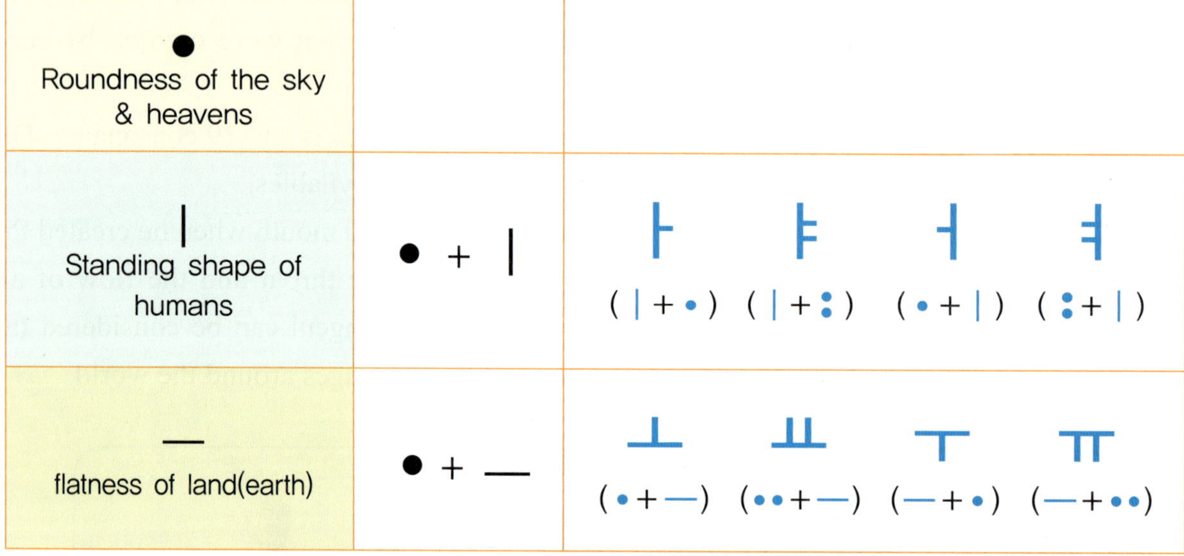

| | | |
|---|---|---|
| ● Roundness of the sky & heavens | | |
| ㅣ Standing shape of humans | ● + ㅣ | ㅏ (ㅣ+•) ㅑ (ㅣ+:) ㅓ (•+ㅣ) ㅕ (:+ㅣ) |
| ㅡ flatness of land(earth) | ● + ㅡ | ㅗ (•+ㅡ) ㅛ (••+ㅡ) ㅜ (ㅡ+•) ㅠ (ㅡ+••) |

Hangeul currently consists of 21 vowels and all of them can be formed by a combination of these three basic representations.

## 2) 모음의 입술모양과 혀의 위치 Formation and Position of the Lips and Tongue for Creating Vowel Sounds

To show the phonetic relations among the sounds represented by the simple vowels, they may be arranged in a chart like the following.

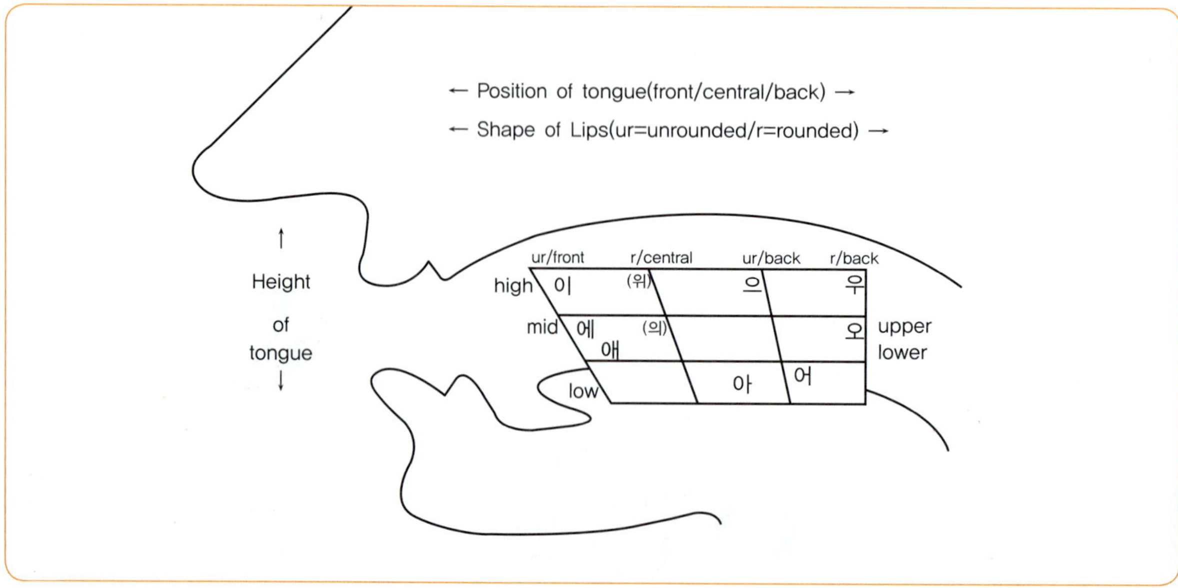

### 3) 21개 모음 The 21 Hangeul Vowel Letters

기본 모음
Basic Vowels

| 글자 Letter | 소리 Sound Value |
|---|---|
| ㅏ | [a] |
| ㅑ | [ya] |
| ㅓ | [eo] |
| ㅕ | [yeo] |
| ㅗ | [o] |
| ㅛ | [yo] |
| ㅜ | [u] |
| ㅠ | [yu] |
| ㅡ | [eu] |
| ㅣ | [i] |

복합 모음
Combined Vowels

| 글자 Letter | 소리 Sound Value | 글자 Letter | 소리 Sound Value | 글자 Letter | 소리 Sound Value |
|---|---|---|---|---|---|
| ㅐ | [ae] | | | | |
| ㅒ | [yae] | | | | |
| ㅔ | [e] | | | | |
| ㅖ | [ye] | | | | |
| ㅘ | [wa] | ㅙ | [wae] | ㅚ | [oe] |
| | | | | | |
| ㅝ | [wo] | ㅞ | [woe] | ㅟ | [wi] |
| | | | | | |
| ㅢ | [ui] | | | | |
| | | | | | |

# Chapter 3 자음 Consonants

There are a total of 19 consonants in Hangeul, and these are divided into 14 basic consonants and 5 combined consonants.

## 1) 자음의 모양 Formation and Position of the Lips and Tongue for Creating Consonant Sounds

The consonants are based on the shape of the voice organs.

① The shape of the tongue root: ㄱ

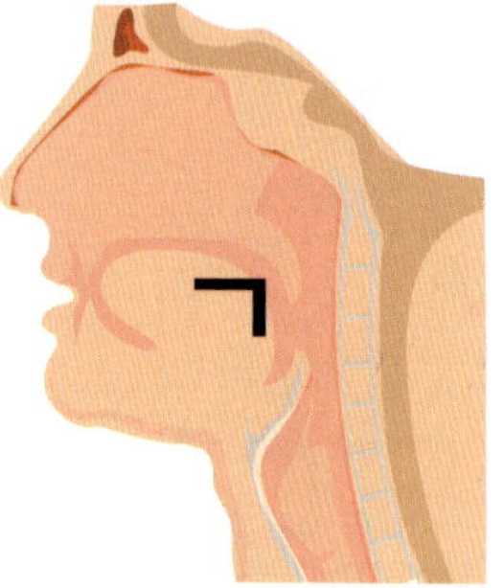


Other consonants are made by adding one or more strokes to the letter: ㅋ

② The shape of the tongue root: ㄴ

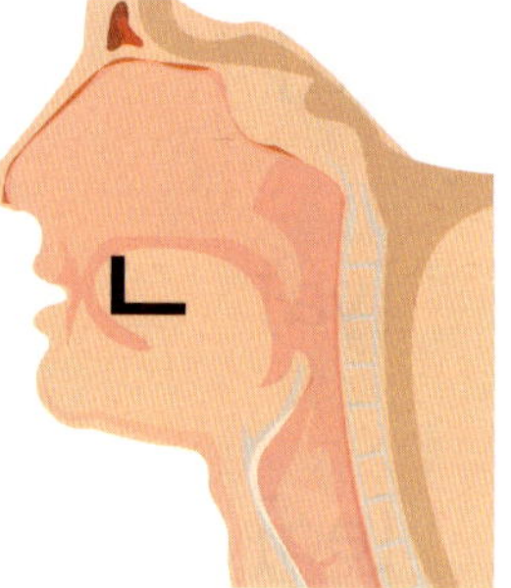


Other consonants are made by adding one or more strokes to the letter: ㄷ, ㅌ, ㄹ

③ The shape of the tongue root: ㅁ

Other consonants are made by adding one or more strokes to the letter: ㅂ, ㅍ

④ The shape of the tongue root: ㅅ

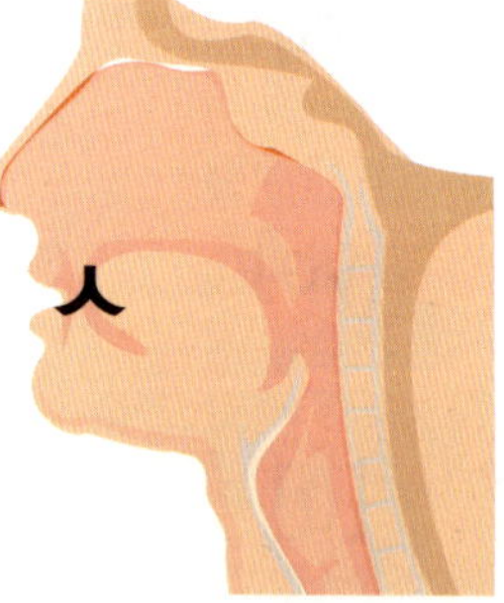


Other consonants are made by adding one or more strokes to the letter: ㅈ, ㅊ

⑤ The shape of the tongue root: ㅇ

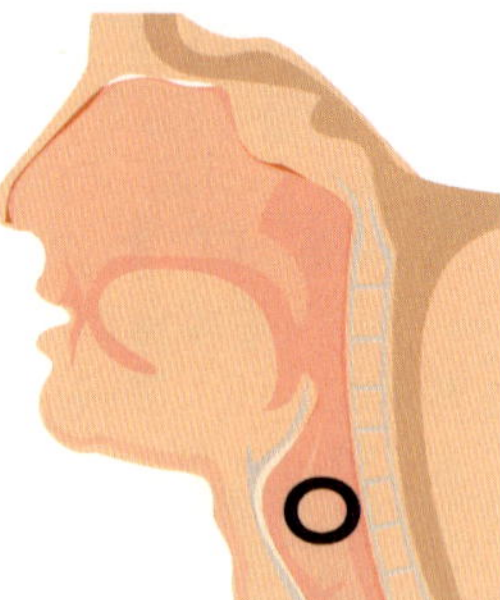


Other consonants are made by adding one or more strokes to the letter: ㅎ

## 2) 19개 자음 The 19 Hangeul Consonant Letters

| 평음 Normal Sounds | | | 격음 Aspirated Sounds | | | 경음 Tensioned Sounds | | |
|---|---|---|---|---|---|---|---|---|
| 글자 Letter | 소리 Sound Value | 이름 Name | 글자 Letter | 소리 Sound Value | 이름 Name | 글자 Letter | 소리 Sound Value | 이름 Name |
| ㄱ | [g,k] | 기역 [giyeok] | ㅋ | [k] | 키읔 [kieuk] | ㄲ | [kk] | 쌍기역 [ssanggiyeok] |
| ㄴ | [n] | 니은 [nieun] | | | | | | |
| ㄷ | [d,t] | 디귿 [digeut] | ㅌ | [t] | 티읕 [tieut] | ㄸ | [tt] | 쌍디귿 [ssangdigeut] |
| ㄹ | [l,r] | 리을 [rieul] | | | | | | |
| ㅁ | [m] | 미음 [mieum] | | | | | | |
| ㅂ | [b,p] | 비읍 [bieup] | ㅍ | [p] | 피읖 [pieup] | ㅃ | [pp] | 쌍비읍 [ssangbieup] |
| ㅅ | [s,sh] | 시옷 [siot] | | | | ㅆ | [ss] | 쌍시옷 [ssangsiot] |
| ㅇ | [ø,ng] | 이응 [ieung] | | | | | | |
| ㅈ | [j,ch] | 지읒 [jieut] | ㅊ | [ch] | 치읓 [chieut] | ㅉ | [jj] | 쌍지읒 [ssangjieut] |
| ㅎ | [h] | 히읗 [hieut] | | | | | | |

Tips

### Names of Consonants

Although Hangeul consonants have individual names, they are difficult to remember; hence at the beginning of Hangeul studies it is best not to memorize Consonant Names individually, but instead try to memorize Consonant Names by the syllables they create when combined with vowels. The following picture on the right illustrates how to easily memorize Consonant Names.

The following green boxes inside the picture are blanks. Once you fill in the blanks with a certain consonant, it creates the name of that consonant. For example, when the consonant 'ㄴ' is written in the blanks, it creates the given Consonant Name on the right. Therefore, the Consonant Name of 'ㄴ' is '니은'. Most of the other Consonant Names can be written by using the same technique. However, the consonants 'ㄱ, ㄷ, are ㅅ' irregular exceptions.

The names of these consonants are '기역, 디귿, and 시옷' respectively, and these should be memorized separately. Also, the five double consonant letters can be named by adding the expression '쌍'(meaning 'double' in Korean) in front of their respective Consonant Names in the singular form.

# Unit Ⅱ

# 한글 Hangeul

# 1 기본모음
## Basic Vowels

### 글자 조합 방법 ① How to Combine Hangeul Letters ①

| V

ㅇ + ㅏ = 아 = 아

Tips

Hangeul is a writing system that combines vowel and consonant units to create syllables. For example, when creating vowel sounds, the consonant "ㅇ" is written in front of the vowel. The consonant 'ㅇ' does not produce any sound when used at the initial position of a syllable, and is only used as a 'filler'. However, when 'ㅇ' is used at the final position of a syllable, hence used as a 'final consonant', it produces the sound [ng].

## 1 기본 모음 익히기 Getting used to Basic Vowels

Listen to the following sounds of vowel letters, and repeat them out loud. Then use Practice 1 to practice writing the given letters by tracing over the outlines, and then use Practice 2 to practice writing the given letters on your own.

| 글자<br>Letter | 소리<br>Sound Value | 쓰기순서<br>Stroke Order | 연습 1<br>Practice 1 | | | 연습 2<br>Practice 2 | | | | |
|---|---|---|---|---|---|---|---|---|---|---|
| ㅏ | [a] | ㅏ | ㅏ | ㅏ | ㅏ | 아 | 아 | | | |
| ㅑ | [ya] | ㅑ | ㅑ | ㅑ | ㅑ | 야 | 야 | | | |
| ㅓ | [eo] | ㅓ | ㅓ | ㅓ | ㅓ | 어 | 어 | | | |
| ㅕ | [yeo] | ㅕ | ㅕ | ㅕ | ㅕ | 여 | 여 | | | |
| ㅗ | [o] | ㅗ | ㅗ | ㅗ | ㅗ | 오 | 오 | | | |
| ㅛ | [yo] | ㅛ | ㅛ | ㅛ | ㅛ | 요 | 요 | | | |
| ㅜ | [u] | ㅜ | ㅜ | ㅜ | ㅜ | 우 | 우 | | | |
| ㅠ | [yu] | ㅠ | ㅠ | ㅠ | ㅠ | 유 | 유 | | | |
| ㅡ | [eu] | ㅡ | ㅡ | ㅡ | ㅡ | 으 | 으 | | | |
| ㅣ | [i] | ㅣ | ㅣ | ㅣ | ㅣ | 이 | 이 | | | |

### Stroke Order of Consonants

Just like in other languages, it is important to learn the correct stroke order of Hangeul letters. If you know the proper stroke order, it will be easier to write and recognize Hangeul letters.

1) Horizontal letters are written from left to right(→).
2) Vertical letters are written from top to bottom(↓).

## 2 연습 Practice

Find the hidden letters, 'ㅏ, ㅑ, ㅓ, ㅕ', within the picture.

Answer page 127

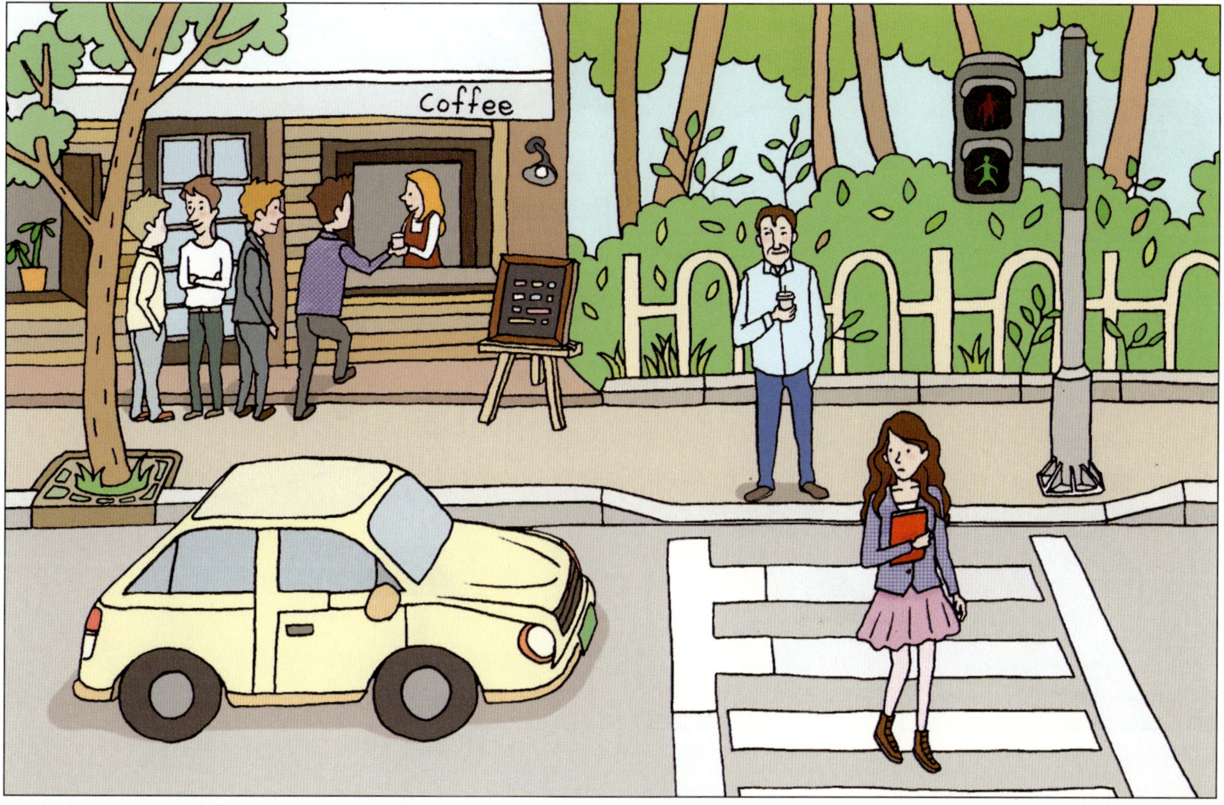


Find the hidden letters, 'ㅗ, ㅛ, ㅜ, ㅠ, ㅡ, ㅣ', within the picture.

Answer page 127

Find the hidden vowels within the picture, and use the empty spaces next to all of the pictures to clearly write the vowel letters.

Find the vowel letters that similar in shape to that of the cookies that the people are holding, and match the vowel letters to the cookies with the same shape.

Match each fisherman/woman with the correct fish and their corresponding vowels, and write the matching vowels in the list below.

| 1 | 2 | 3 | 4 | 5 | 6 | 7 | 8 | 9 | 10 |
| --- | --- | --- | --- | --- | --- | --- | --- | --- | --- |
| 어 | | | | | | | | | |

Listen to the following words. Then read the words out loud, and write it down.

track 02

| 오 | | | | | |
|---|---|---|---|---|---|
| 오 | | | | | |

| 이 | | | | | |
|---|---|---|---|---|---|
| 이 | | | | | |

| 아 | 이 | | | | |
|---|---|---|---|---|---|
| 아 | 이 | | | | |

| 아 | 우 | | | | |
|---|---|---|---|---|---|
| 아 | 우 | | | | |

| 오 | 이 | | | | |
|---|---|---|---|---|---|
| 오 | 이 | | | | |

| 우 | 유 | | | | |
|---|---|---|---|---|---|
| 우 | 유 | | | | |

| 여 | 우 | | | | |
|---|---|---|---|---|---|
| 여 | 우 | | | | |

# 2 자 음
Consonants

## 글자 조합 방법 ② How to Combine Hangeul Letters ②

### C + V

| C V | ㄴ | + | ㅏ | = | 나 | = | 나 |
|---|---|---|---|---|---|---|---|
| C / V | ㄷ | + | ㅗ | = | 도 | = | 도 |

## 1 자음 익히기 Getting used to Consonants

자음1 ㄱ,ㄴ,ㄷ,ㄹ

Use Practice 1 to practice writing the given letters by tracing over the outlines, and then use Practice 2 to practice writing the given letters on your own.

| 글자 Letter | 소리 Sound Value | 이름 Name | 쓰기순서 Stroke Order | 연습 1 Practice 1 | 연습 2 Practice 2 | | | |
|---|---|---|---|---|---|---|---|---|
| ㄱ | [g,k]* | 기역 [giyeok] | ㄱ ① | ㄱ ㄱ ㄱ | | | | |
| ㄴ | [n] | 니은 [nieun] | ① ㄴ | ㄴ ㄴ ㄴ | | | | |
| ㄷ | [d,t]** | 디귿 [digeut] | ① ② ㄷ | ㄷ ㄷ ㄷ | | | | |
| ㄹ | [l,r]*** | 리을 [rieul] | ① ② ③ ㄹ | ㄹ ㄹ ㄹ | | | | |

• * If the consonant letter 'ㄱ' is placed between two different vowel letters as demonstrated in this picture, it produces a sound similar to [g].

ex 

• ** If the consonant letter 'ㄷ' is placed between two different vowel letters as demonstrated in this picture, it produces a sound similar to [d].

ex 

• *** If the consonant letter 'ㄹ' is placed between two different vowel letters as demonstrated in this picture, it produces a sound similar to [r].

ex 

Listen to the following sounds of syllables created by combining consonant and vowel letters, and repeat them out loud. Then practice combining consonant and vowel letters to create syllables on your own.

| 모음 / 자음 | ㅏ | ㅑ | ㅓ | ㅕ | ㅗ | ㅛ | ㅜ | ㅠ | ㅡ | ㅣ |
|---|---|---|---|---|---|---|---|---|---|---|
| ㄱ | *가 | | | | *고 | | | | | |
| ㄴ | | | | | | 뇨 | | | | |
| ㄷ | | 댜 | | | | | | | | |
| ㄹ | | | | | | | 루 | | | |

- The consonants are only pronounced when combined with vowels. Combine the vowels and consonants to make syllables.
- * When writing the consonant 'ㄱ' on the right side of a syllable, the letter should be written with a slight curvature like this "ㄱ". However, when writing the consonant 'ㄱ' at the bottom of a syllable, the letter should be written with no curvature.

Find the hidden letters, 'ㄱ, ㄴ, ㄷ, ㄹ', within the picture.

Answer next page

Study the letters found in 'Picture 1', and try to mimic the given letters by following the body postures in 'Picture 2'.

Listen to the following words. Then read the words out loud, and write it down. track 04

| | | | | | |
|---|---|---|---|---|---|
| 야 | 구 | | | | |
| 야 | 구 | | | | |
| 고 | 기 | | | | |
| 고 | 기 | | | | |
| 나 | 이 | | | | |
| 나 | 이 | | | | |
| 누 | 나 | | | | |
| 누 | 나 | | | | |
| 구 | 두 | | | | |
| 구 | 두 | | | | |
| 다 | 리 | | | | |
| 다 | 리 | | | | |

오리
오리
가구
가구
Here
여기
여기
너
너
아니요
아니요
나누다
나누다

Here
오 다
오 다
기 러 기
기 러 기

Listen and find the corresponding words, and match them with the correct pictures. Then, re-write the words.

구

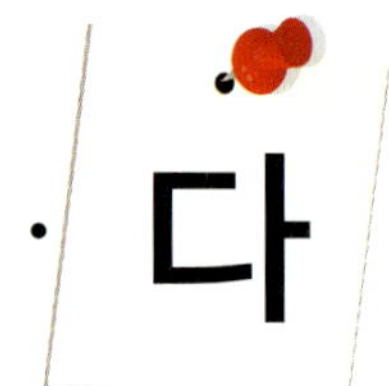


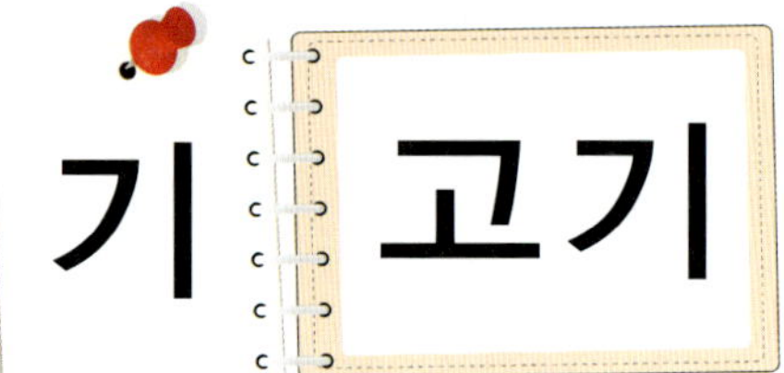

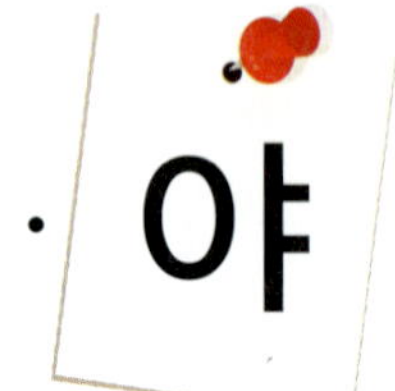

## 자음2 ㅁ,ㅂ,ㅅ,ㅇ,ㅈ

Use Practice 1 to practice writing the given letters by tracing over the outlines, and then use Practice 2 to practice writing the given letters on your own.

| 글자<br>Letter | 소리<br>Sound Value | 이름<br>Name | 쓰기순서<br>Stroke order | 연 습 1<br>Practice 1 | 연 습 2<br>Practice 2 | | | |
|---|---|---|---|---|---|---|---|---|
| ㅁ | [m] | 미음<br>[mieum] | ① ② ③ | ㅁ ㅁ ㅁ | | | | |
| ㅂ | [b,p]* | 비읍<br>[bieup] | ① ② ③ ④ | ㅂ ㅂ ㅂ | | | | |
| ㅅ | [s,sh]** | 시옷<br>[siot] | ① ② | ㅅ ㅅ ㅅ | | | | |
| ㅇ | [ø,ng]*** | 이응<br>[ieung] | ① | ㅇ ㅇ ㅇ | | | | |
| ㅈ**** | [j,ch] | 지읒<br>[jieut] | ① ② ③ | ㅈ ㅈ ㅈ | | | | |

- * If the consonant letter 'ㅂ' is placed between two different vowel letters as demonstrated in this picture, it produces a sound similar to [b].

- ** When the letter 'ㅅ' is combined with the one of the following vowels 'ㅑ, ㅕ, ㅛ, ㅠ, ㅣ' it is pronounced [sh]. The letter 'ㅅ' can be written in various styles such as 'ㅅ ㅅ ㅅ ㅅ ㅅ'.
- *** If the letter 'ㅇ' is placed in the initial position of a syllable, it has no sound value. However, if it is placed in the final position of a syllable, it is pronounced like [ng] in English. The letter 'ㅇ' can be written in various styles such as 'ㅇ ㅇ ㅇ ㅇ ㅇ'.
- **** The letter 'ㅈ' can be written in various styles such as 'ㅈ ㅈ ㅈ ㅈ ㅈ'.

Listen to the following sounds of syllables created by combining consonant and vowel letters, and repeat them out loud. Then practice combining consonant and vowel letters to create syllables on your own.

| 모음 / 자음 | ㅏ | ㅑ | ㅓ | ㅕ | ㅗ | ㅛ | ㅜ | ㅠ | ㅡ | ㅣ |
|---|---|---|---|---|---|---|---|---|---|---|
| ㅁ | | 먀 | | | | | | | | |
| ㅂ | | | 버 | | | | | | | |
| ㅅ | | | | | | | 수 | | | |
| ㅇ | | | | 여 | | | | | | |
| ㅈ | | | | | | | | | 즈 | |

• The shaded areas indicate pronunciations that do not exist in the Korean language.

Find the hidden letters, 'ㅁ, ㅂ, ㅅ, ㅇ, ㅈ', within the picture.

Study the letters found in 'Picture 1', and try to mimic the given letters by following the body postures in 'Picture 2'.

Listen to the following words. Then read the words out loud, and write it down.

track 07

| 나 | 무 | | | | |
|---|---|---|---|---|---|
| 나 | 무 | | | | |
| 머 | 리 | | | | |
| 머 | 리 | | | | |
| 비 | 누 | | | | |
| 비 | 누 | | | | |
| 나 | 비 | | | | |
| 나 | 비 | | | | |
| 서 | 다 | | | | |
| 서 | 다 | | | | |
| 버 | 스 | | | | |
| 버 | 스 | | | | |

모자
모자
거미
거미
모기
모기
바구니
바구니
바나나
바나나
사다리
사다리

소리
소리
여자
여자

Listen and find the corresponding words, and match them with the correct pictures. Then, re-write the words.

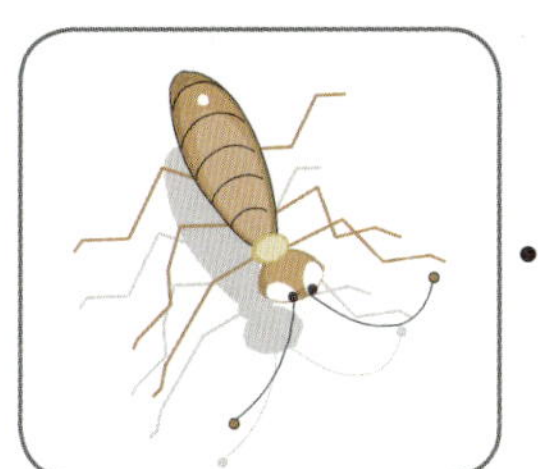

## 자음3 ㅊ,ㅋ,ㅌ,ㅍ,ㅎ

Use Practice 1 to practice writing the given letters by tracing over the outlines, and then use Practice 2 to practice writing the given letters on your own.

| 글자 Letter | 소리 Sound Value | 이름 Name | 쓰기순서 Stroke order | 연습 1 Practice 1 | 연습 2 Practice 2 |
|---|---|---|---|---|---|
| ㅊ* | [ch] | 치읓 [chieut] | ㅊ | ㅊ ㅊ ㅊ | |
| ㅋ | [k] | 키읔 [kieuk] | ㅋ | ㅋ ㅋ ㅋ | |
| ㅌ | [t] | 티읕 [tieut] | ㅌ | ㅌ ㅌ ㅌ | |
| ㅍ | [p] | 피읖 [pieup] | ㅍ | ㅍ ㅍ ㅍ | |
| ㅎ** | [h] | 히읗 [hieut] | ㅎ | ㅎ ㅎ ㅎ | |

- * The letter 'ㅊ' can be written in various styles such as 'ㅊ ㅊ ㅊ ㅊ ㅊ'.
- ** The letter 'ㅎ' can be written in various styles such as 'ㅎ ㅎ ㅎ ㅎ ㅎ'.

Listen to the following sounds of syllables created by combining consonant and vowel letters, and repeat them out loud. Then practice combining consonant and vowel letters to create syllables on your own.

track 09

| 모음 / 자음 | ㅏ | ㅑ | ㅓ | ㅕ | ㅗ | ㅛ | ㅜ | ㅠ | ㅡ | ㅣ |
|---|---|---|---|---|---|---|---|---|---|---|
| ㅊ | | | 처 | | | | | | | |
| ㅋ | | | | 켜 | | | | | | |
| ㅌ | | | | | | | | 튜 | | |
| ㅍ | | | | | | | | | 프 | |
| ㅎ | | | | | | | | | | 히 |

- The shaded areas indicate pronunciations that do not exist in the Korean language.

Find the hidden letters, 'ㅊ, ㅋ, ㅌ, ㅍ, ㅎ' within the picture.

Answer next page

Study the letters found in 'Picture 1', and try to mimic the given letters by following the body postures in 'Picture 2'.

Listen to the following words. Then read the words out loud, and write it down. track 10

| 고 | 추 | | | | |
|---|---|---|---|---|---|
| 고 | 추 | | | | |
| 치 | 마 | | | | |
| 치 | 마 | | | | |
| 기 | 차 | | | | |
| 기 | 차 | | | | |
| 키 | | | | | |
| 키 | | | | | |
| 크 | 다 | | | | |
| 크 | 다 | | | | |
| 코 | 트 | | | | |
| 코 | 트 | | | | |

| | | | | | |
|---|---|---|---|---|---|
| 커 | 피 | | | | |
| 커 | 피 | | | | |
| 타 | 다 | | | | |
| 타 | 다 | | | | |
| 투 | 수 | | | | |
| 투 | 수 | | | | |
| 티 | 셔 | 츠 | | | |
| 티 | 셔 | 츠 | | | |
| 아 | 프 | 다 | | | |
| 아 | 프 | 다 | | | |
| 포 | 도 | | | | |
| 포 | 도 | | | | |

| 하 | 나 | | | | |
|---|---|---|---|---|---|
| 하 | 나 | | | | |

| 지 | 하 | | | | |
|---|---|---|---|---|---|
| 지 | 하 | | | | |

Listen and find the corresponding words, and match them with the correct pictures. Then, re-write the words.

Use Practice 1 to practice writing the given letters by tracing over the outlines, and then use Practice 2 to practice writing the given letters on your own.

| 글자 Letter | 소리 Sound Value | 이름 Name | 쓰기순서 Stroke order | 연습 1 Practice 1 | 연습 2 Practice 2 | | | |
|---|---|---|---|---|---|---|---|---|
| ㄲ | [kk] | 쌍기역 [ssanggiyeok] | ㄲ | ㄲ ㄲ ㄲ | | | | |
| ㄸ | [tt] | 쌍디귿 [ssangdigeut] | ㄸ | ㄸ ㄸ ㄸ | | | | |
| ㅃ | [pp] | 쌍비읍 [ssangbieup] | ㅃ | ㅃ ㅃ ㅃ | | | | |
| ㅆ | [ss] | 쌍시옷 [ssangsiot] | ㅆ | ㅆ ㅆ ㅆ | | | | |
| ㅉ | [jj] | 쌍지읒 [ssangjieut] | ㅉ | ㅉ ㅉ ㅉ | | | | |

Listen to the following sounds of syllables created by combining consonant and vowel letters, and repeat them out loud. Then practice combining consonant and vowel letters to create syllables on your own.

| 모음 / 자음 | ㅏ | ㅑ | ㅓ | ㅕ | ㅗ | ㅛ | ㅜ | ㅠ | ㅡ | ㅣ |
|---|---|---|---|---|---|---|---|---|---|---|
| ㄲ | 까 | | | | | | | | | |
| ㄸ | | | 떠 | | | | | | | |
| ㅃ | | | | | | 뾰 | | | | |
| ㅆ | | | | | | | 쑤 | | | |
| ㅉ | | | | | | | | | 쯔 | |

Tips

- The consonants written with double letters are each single sounds.
- The shaded areas indicate pronunciations that do not exist in the Korean language.

The following pronunciations are difficult to distinguish. Practice reading them out loud several times.

track 13

① 그다 / 크다 / 끄다 ② 고리 / 꼬리 ③ 도끼 / 토끼 / 또기 ④ 다르다 / 따르다
⑤ 바다 / 파다 / 빠다 ⑥ 바르다 / 빠르다 ⑦ 사다 / 싸다 ⑧ 서다 / 쓰다
⑨ 자다 / 차다 / 짜다 ⑩ 가치 / 까치

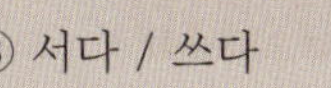

Listen to the following words. Then read the words out loud, and write it down. track 14

| | | | | | | |
|---|---|---|---|---|---|---|
| 까 | 치 | | | | |
| 까 | 치 | | | | |
| 꼬 | 리 | | | | |
| 꼬 | 리 | | | | |
| 따 | 다 | | | | |
| 따 | 다 | | | | |
| 로 | 또 | | | | |
| 로 | 또 | | | | |
| 아 | 빠 | | | | |
| 아 | 빠 | | | | |
| 뽀 | 뽀 | | | | |
| 뽀 | 뽀 | | | | |

₩ 50,000,000
비싸다
비싸다
Vintage Flower
쓰다
쓰다
SALT
짜다
짜다
코끼리
코끼리
머리띠
머리띠
따르다
따르다

뿌리
바쁘다
싸우다
아가씨
가짜
찌르다

Listen and find the corresponding words, and match them with the correct pictures. Then, re-write the words.

| | | |
|---|---|---|
|  가 | 빠 | 아빠 |
|  아 | 뽀 | |
|  로 | 다 | |
|  쓰 | 리 | |
|  뿌 | 짜 | |
|  뽀 | 또 | |

## 2 연습 Practice

The following list displays the proper order of Basic Vowels and Consonants. Listen and follow along with the order to complete the picture.

아 → 야 → 어 → 여 → 오 → 요 → 우 → 유 → 으 → 이 → 가 → 나 →
다 → 라 → 마 → 바 → 사 → 아 → 자 → 차 → 카 → 타 → 파 → 하

Answer page 128

Practice combining consonant and vowel letters to create syllables on your own.

| 모음 / 자음 | ㅏ | ㅑ | ㅓ | ㅕ | ㅗ | ㅛ | ㅜ | ㅠ | ㅡ | ㅣ |
|---|---|---|---|---|---|---|---|---|---|---|
| ㄱ | 가 | | | | | | | | | |
| ㄴ | | | | | 노 | | | | | |
| ㄷ | | 댜 | | | | | | | | |
| ㄹ | | | 러 | | | | | | | |
| ㅁ | | | | 며 | | | | | | |
| ㅂ | | | | | 보 | | | | | |
| ㅅ | | | | | | 쇼 | | | | |
| ㅇ | | | | | | | 우 | | | |
| ㅈ | | | | | | | | | 즈 | |
| ㅊ | | | | | | | | | 츠 | |
| ㅋ | | | | | | | | | | 키 |
| ㅌ | 타 | | | | | | | | | |
| ㅍ | | 퍄 | | | | | | | | |
| ㅎ | | | 허 | | | | | | | |

· The shaded areas indicate pronunciations that do not exist in the Korean language.

| 모음<br>자음 | ㅏ | ㅑ | ㅓ | ㅕ | ㅗ | ㅛ | ㅜ | ㅠ | ㅡ | ㅣ |
|---|---|---|---|---|---|---|---|---|---|---|
| ㄲ | | | | 껴 | | | | | | |
| ㄸ | | | | | 또 | | | | | |
| ㅃ | | | | | | 뾰 | | | | |
| ㅆ | | | | | | | 쑤 | | | |
| ㅉ | | | | | | | | 쮸 | | |

· The shaded areas indicate pronunciations that do not exist in the Korean language.

Listen to the following statement as you observe the given picture, and fill in the blank with the correct name of the consonant.

track 17

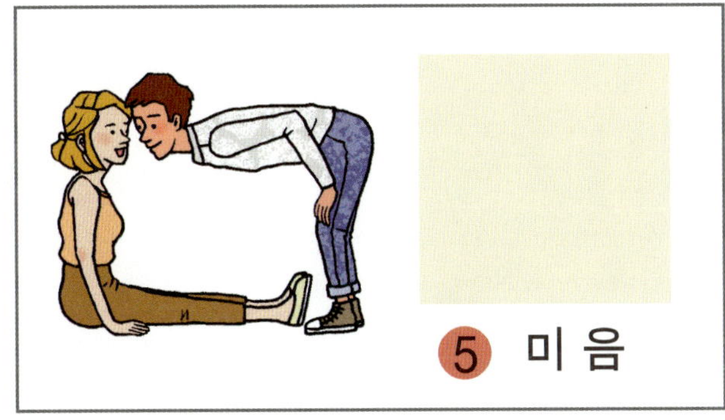
5 미음

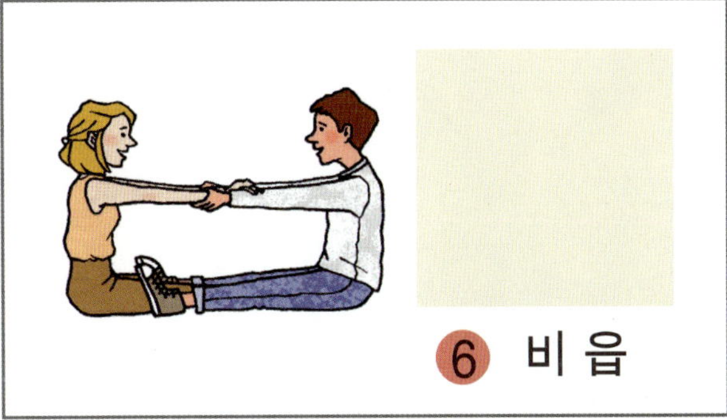
6 비읍

7 시옷

8 이응

9 지읒

10 치읓

11 키읔

12 티읕

13 피읖

14 히읗

# 3
# 복합모음
## Combined Vowels

## 1 복합 모음 익히기 Getting used to Combined Vowels

Use Practice 1 to practice writing the given letters by tracing over the outlines, and then use Practice 2 to practice writing the given letters on your own.

| 글자 Letter | 소리 Sound Value | 쓰기순서 Stroke order | 연습 1 Practice 1 | | | 연습 2 Practice 2 | | | |
|---|---|---|---|---|---|---|---|---|---|
| ㅔ* | [e] | | ㅔ | ㅔ | ㅔ | 에 | | | |
| ㅐ* | [ae] | | ㅐ | ㅐ | ㅐ | 애 | | | |
| ㅖ** | [yae] | | ㅖ | ㅖ | ㅖ | 예 | | | |
| ㅒ** | [ye] | | ㅒ | ㅒ | ㅒ | 얘 | | | |
| ㅘ | [wa] | | ㅘ | ㅘ | ㅘ | 와 | | | |
| ㅝ | [weo] | | ㅝ | ㅝ | ㅝ | 워 | | | |
| ㅙ*** | [wae] | | ㅙ | ㅙ | ㅙ | 왜 | | | |
| ㅚ*** | [oe] | | ㅚ | ㅚ | ㅚ | 외 | | | |
| ㅞ*** | [we] | | ㅞ | ㅞ | ㅞ | 웨 | | | |
| ㅟ | [wi] | | ㅟ | ㅟ | ㅟ | 위 | | | |
| ㅢ**** | [ui] | | ㅢ | ㅢ | ㅢ | 의 | | | |

- The pronunciations between the letters *‘ㅐ’ and ‘ㅔ’, **‘ㅒ’ and ‘ㅖ’, and ***'ㅚ, ㅙ and ㅞ' differ only in standard Korean speech nowadays.
- The pronunciation of ****'ㅢ'
  1) ㅢ → [ㅢ]
     When 'ㅢ' is located at the first syllable of a word, and there is no consonant in the syllable before ㅢ, ㅢ is always pronounced [ㅢ]. Example: 의자[의자] 의사[의사]
  2) ㅢ → [ㅣ]
     When ㅢ is located at the final syllable of a word, or when ㅢ is located at the final syllable of a word after a consonant in the syllable before ㅢ, ㅢ can be pronounced [I]. Example : 회의[회이 / 회의] 무늬[무니 / 무늬]

Listen to the following words. Then read the words out loud, and write it down. track 18

| 그 | 네 | | | | |
|---|---|---|---|---|---|
| 그 | 네 | | | | |

| 개 | 미 | | | | |
|---|---|---|---|---|---|
| 개 | 미 | | | | |

| 얘 | 기 | | | | |
|---|---|---|---|---|---|
| 얘 | 기 | | | | |

| 시 | 계 | | | | |
|---|---|---|---|---|---|
| 시 | 계 | | | | |

| 사 | 과 | | | | |
|---|---|---|---|---|---|
| 사 | 과 | | | | |

| 돼 | 지 | | | | |
|---|---|---|---|---|---|
| 돼 | 지 | | | | |

교회
교회
세수
세수
세다
세다
무지개
무지개
해바라기
해바라기
화가
화가

| | | | | | |
|---|---|---|---|---|---|
| 회 | 사 | | | | |
| 회 | 사 | | | | |

| | | | | | |
|---|---|---|---|---|---|
| 열 | 쇠 | | | | |
| 열 | 쇠 | | | | |

| | | | | | |
|---|---|---|---|---|---|
| 샤 | 워 | | | | |
| 샤 | 워 | | | | |

| | | | | | |
|---|---|---|---|---|---|
| 뛰 | 다 | | | | |
| 뛰 | 다 | | | | |

| | | | | | |
|---|---|---|---|---|---|
| 쥐 | | | | | |
| 쥐 | | | | | |

| | | | | | |
|---|---|---|---|---|---|
| 가 | 위 | | | | |
| 가 | 위 | | | | |

주 사 위
의 사
스 웨 터

Listen and find the corresponding words, and match them with the correct pictures. Then, re-write the words.

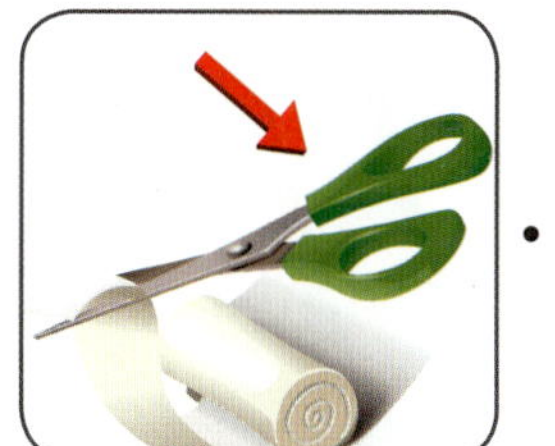

## 2 연습 Practice

The following list demonstrates how vowels are properly ordered and listed in dictionaries. Listen and follow along with the order to complete the maze.

아 → 애 → 야 → 얘 → 어 → 에 → 여 → 예 → 오 → 와 → 왜 → 외 → 요 → 우 → 워 → 웨 → 위 → 유 → 으 → 의 → 이

Answer page 128

The following list demonstrates how vowels and consonants are properly ordered and listed in dictionaries. Listen and follow along with the order to complete the picture. track 22

아 → 애 → 야 → 얘 → 어 → 에 → 여 → 예 → 오 → 와 → 왜 → 외 → 요 → 우 → 워 → 웨 → 위 → 유 → 으 → 의 → 이 → 가 → 까 → 나 → 다 → 따 → 라 → 마 → 바 → 빠 → 사 → 싸 → 아 → 자 → 짜 → 차 → 카 → 타 → 파 → 하

Practice combining consonant and vowel letters to create syllables on your own.

| 모음 / 자음 | ㅔ | ㅐ | ㅖ | ㅒ | ㅘ | ㅝ | ㅙ | ㅚ | ㅞ | ㅟ | ㅢ |
|---|---|---|---|---|---|---|---|---|---|---|---|
| ㄱ | 게 | | | | | | | | | | |
| ㄴ | | | | | 놔 | | | | | | |
| ㄷ | | | | | | | | | | | |
| ㄹ | | | | | | | | | | | |
| ㅁ | | | | | | | | | | | |
| ㅂ | | | | | | | | | | | |
| ㅅ | | | | | | | | | | | |
| ㅇ | | | | | | | | | | | |
| ㅈ | | | | | | | | | | | |
| ㅊ | | | | | | | | | | | |
| ㅋ | | | | | | | | | | | |
| ㅌ | | | | | | | | | | | |
| ㅍ | | | | | | | | | | | |
| ㅎ | | | | | | | | | | | |

| 모음 / 자음 | ㅔ | ㅐ | ㅖ | ㅒ | ㅘ | ㅝ | ㅙ | ㅚ | ㅞ | ㅟ | ㅢ |
|---|---|---|---|---|---|---|---|---|---|---|---|
| ㄲ | | | | | | | | | | | |
| ㄸ | | | | | | | | | | | |
| ㅃ | | | | | | | | | | | |
| ㅆ | | | | | | | | | | | |
| ㅉ | | | | | | | | | | | |

· The shaded areas indicate pronunciations that do not exist in the Korean language.

# 4 받침
Final consonants

## 글자 조합 방법 ③ How to Combine Hangeul Letters ③

### C + V + C

| | | | | | | | | |
|---|---|---|---|---|---|---|---|---|
| C V / C | ㄱ | + | ㅏ | + | ㅇ | = | 강 | 강 |
| C / V / C | ㄷ | + | ㅗ | + | ㄴ | = | 돈 | 돈 |

### C + V + C + C

| | | | | | | | | | | |
|---|---|---|---|---|---|---|---|---|---|---|
| C V / C C | ㄱ | + | ㅏ | + | ㅂ | + | ㅅ | = | 값 | 값 |
| C / V / C C | ㅎ | + | ㅡ | + | ㄹ | + | ㄱ | = | 흙 | 흙 |

## 1 받침 익히기 Getting used to Final Consonants

In Korean, consonants are used at the beginning of a syllable, as well as at the end of it. All consonant letters can be used as final consonants, but there are only 7 consonant sounds that can be heard at the end of a syllable. These consonant sounds are [ㄱ, ㄴ, ㄷ, ㄹ, ㅁ, ㅂ, ㅇ]. If any other consonants come at the end of a syllable, the sound of the final consonant is changed into one of the 7 consonants.

| 받침글자 Letter | 소 리 Sound Value | 예 Example |
|---|---|---|
| ㄱ | [-k] | 약, 가족, 대학 |
| ㅋ | | 부엌 |
| ㄲ | | 밖, 낚시 |
| ㄴ | [-n] | 눈, 친구, 자전거 |
| ㄹ | [-l] | 말, 서울, 불고기 |
| ㅁ | [-m] | 사람, 이름 |
| ㅂ, ㅍ | [-p] | 집, 입, 잎, 앞 |
| ㅇ | [-ng] | 강, 빵, 선생님 |
| ㄷ, ㅌ | [-t] | 듣다, 곧, 끝, 밑 |
| ㅅ, ㅆ | | 낫, 옷, 있다 |
| ㅈ, ㅊ | | 낮, 낯 |
| ㅎ | | 히읗 |
| ㄳ ㄶ<br>ㄵ ㄼ<br>ㄾ ㅄ | * The consonant on the left is pronounced for these cases. | 몫, 많다, 앉다, 여덟, 넓다, 값, 없다 |
| ㄺ, ㄻ, ㄿ | ** The consonant on the right is pronounced for these cases. | 흙, 읽다, 젊다, 삶다, 읊다 |

- * It is possible to have a syllable with two consonant letters filling the final position.
- ** They may be two different consonant letters. Some reduce to the first consonant, some to the last.

### Pronunciation of Final Consonants

When a batchim(final consonant) of a syllable is followed by a syllable that begins with a vowel, the batchim is pronounced as if it were in the position of that vowel. This is called "liaison".

한국어 [한구거]　음악 [으막]　발음[바름]
월요일[워료일]　직업[지겁]

## 받침1 ㄱ,ㅋ,ㄲ / ㄴ,ㄹ,ㅁ

Listen to the following words. Then read the words out loud, and write it down.

| 맥 | 주 | | | | |
|---|---|---|---|---|---|
| 맥 | 주 | | | | |

| 가 | 족 | | | | |
|---|---|---|---|---|---|
| 가 | 족 | | | | |

| 치 | 약 | | | | |
|---|---|---|---|---|---|
| 치 | 약 | | | | |

| 학 | 교 | | | | |
|---|---|---|---|---|---|
| 학 | 교 | | | | |

| 부 | 엌 | | | | |
|---|---|---|---|---|---|
| 부 | 엌 | | | | |

깎 다
깎 다

낚 시
낚 시

산
산

돈
돈

말
말

연 필
연 필

얼굴
얼굴
남자
남자
인삼
인삼

Listen and find the corresponding words, and match them with the correct pictures. Then, re-write the words.

## 받침2 ㅂ,ㅍ,ㅇ

Listen to the following words. Then read the words out loud, and write it down. track 25

| 집 | | | | | |
|---|---|---|---|---|---|
| 집 | | | | | |

| 잡 | 지 | | | | |
|---|---|---|---|---|---|
| 잡 | 지 | | | | |

| 무 | 릎 | | | | |
|---|---|---|---|---|---|
| 무 | 릎 | | | | |

| 지 | 갑 | | | | |
|---|---|---|---|---|---|
| 지 | 갑 | | | | |

| 가 | 방 | | | | |
|---|---|---|---|---|---|
| 가 | 방 | | | | |

앞
앞
학 생
학 생
선 생 님
선 생 님

Listen and find the corresponding words, and match them with the correct pictures. Then, re-write the words.

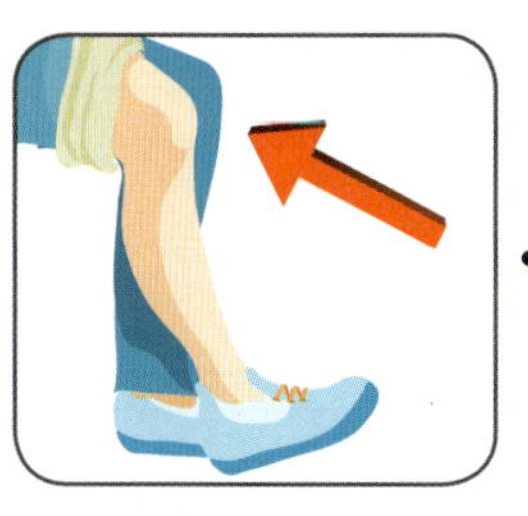

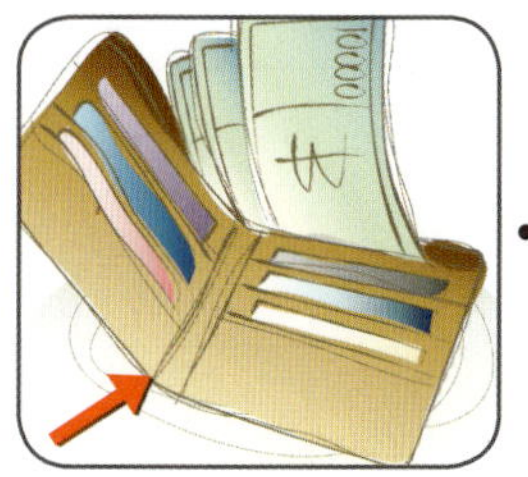

받침3 ㄷ,ㅌ,ㅅ,ㅆ,ㅈ,ㅊ,ㅎ

Listen to the following words. Then read the words out loud, and write it down.

| | | | | | |
|---|---|---|---|---|---|
| 걷 | 다 | | | | |
| 걷 | 다 | | | | |

| | | | | | |
|---|---|---|---|---|---|
| 듣 | 다 | | | | |
| 듣 | 다 | | | | |

| | | | | | |
|---|---|---|---|---|---|
| 숟 | 가 | 락 | | | |
| 숟 | 가 | 락 | | | |

| | | | | | |
|---|---|---|---|---|---|
| 돋 | 보 | 기 | | | |
| 돋 | 보 | 기 | | | |

| | | | | | |
|---|---|---|---|---|---|
| 밭 | | | | | |
| 밭 | | | | | |

| | | | | | |
|---|---|---|---|---|---|
| 다 | 섯 | | | | |
| 다 | 섯 | | | | |

| 칫 | 솔 | | | | |
|---|---|---|---|---|---|
| 칫 | 솔 | | | | |

| 버 | 섯 | | | | |
|---|---|---|---|---|---|
| 버 | 섯 | | | | |

| 젓 | 가 | 락 | | | |
|---|---|---|---|---|---|
| 젓 | 가 | 락 | | | |

| 낮 | | | | | |
|---|---|---|---|---|---|
| 낮 | | | | | |

| 낮 | 잠 | | | | |
|---|---|---|---|---|---|
| 낮 | 잠 | | | | |

| 햇 | 빛 | | | | |
|---|---|---|---|---|---|
| 햇 | 빛 | | | | |

| 꽃 | | | | | |
|---|---|---|---|---|---|
| 꽃 | | | | | |

ㅎ

| 히 | 읗 | | | | |
|---|---|---|---|---|---|
| 히 | 읗 | | | | |

Listen and find the corresponding words, and match them with the correct pictures. Then, re-write the words.

| | | | |
|---|---|---|---|
| | 히 | 솔 | |
| | 낮 | 읗 | |
| | 햇 | 섯 | |
| ㅎ | 걷 | 다 | 걷다 |
| | 버 | 빛 | |
| | 칫 | 잠 | |

## 받침4 ㄳ, ㄶ, ㄵ, ㄼ, ㄾ, ㅄ, ㄺ, ㄻ, ㄿ

Listen to the following words. Then read the words out loud, and write it down. track 29

| 8 | 여 | 덟 | | | | |
|---|---|---|---|---|---|---|
| | 여 | 덟 | | | | |
| | 닭 | | | | | |
| | 닭 | | | | | |
| | 읽 | 다 | | | | |
| | 읽 | 다 | | | | |
| | 앉 | 다 | | | | |
| | 앉 | 다 | | | | |
|  | 많 | 다 | | | | |
| | 많 | 다 | | | | |

넓 다
넓 다
값
값
10000
10000
10000

## 2 연습 Practice

Find the following Vocabulary Words in the Word Search Exercise below, and circle or highlight the words accordingly.

Answer page 129

**Examples** 한국, 한국어

**Hidden Words** 가족, 태극기, 자전거, 가방, 선생님, 장미, 숟가락, 여덟, 다섯, 많다, 부엌, 얼굴, 엄마, 고향

Examples

| | | | | | | | |
|---|---|---|---|---|---|---|---|
| 나 | 다 | 섯 | 의 | 살 | 한 | 국 | 던 |
| 얼 | 던 | 고 | 향 | 은 | 국 | 꽃 | 피 |
| 굴 | 산 | 가 | 족 | 골 | 어 | 복 | 숭 |
| 아 | 꽃 | 살 | 구 | 꽃 | 아 | 기 | 진 |
| 가 | 달 | 엄 | 울 | 여 | 긋 | 불 | 자 |
| 방 | 긋 | 마 | 대 | 덟 | 궐 | 차 | 전 |
| 리 | 부 | 힌 | 동 | 네 | 그 | 속 | 거 |
| 에 | 엌 | 서 | 많 | 놀 | 던 | 때 | 가 |
| 그 | 립 | 습 | 다 | 니 | 선 | 생 | 님 |
| 다 | 장 | 미 | 꽃 | 동 | 네 | 새 | 동 |
| 네 | 나 | 의 | 옛 | 숟 | 가 | 락 | 고 |
| 향 | 태 | 극 | 기 | 파 | 란 | 들 | 남 |

# 서바이벌 한국어 Survival Korean

# 1 한국어 인사말
Greetings

Listen to the dialog, Then read the dialog out loud, and write it down.

A 안녕하세요?
Hello.

B 안녕하세요?
Hello.

| 안 | 녕 | 하 | 세 | 요 | ? |
|---|---|---|---|---|---|
| | | | | | |
| | | | | | |

A 만나서 반갑습니다.
Nice to meet you.

B 만나서 반갑습니다.
Nice to meet you.

| 만 | 나 | 서 | | 반 | 갑 | 습 | 니 | 다 | . |
|---|---|---|---|---|---|---|---|---|---|
| | | | | | | | | | |
| | | | | | | | | | |

A 안녕히 가세요.
Goodbye.
(to the person who is leaving)

B 안녕히 계세요.
Goodbye.
(to the person who is staying)

| 안 | 녕 | 히 |  | 가 | 세 | 요 | . |
|---|---|---|---|---|---|---|---|
|  |  |  |  |  |  |  |  |
|  |  |  |  |  |  |  |  |

| 안 | 녕 | 히 |  | 계 | 세 | 요 | . |
|---|---|---|---|---|---|---|---|
|  |  |  |  |  |  |  |  |
|  |  |  |  |  |  |  |  |

A 안녕히 가세요.
Goodbye.

B 안녕히 가세요.
Goodbye.

| 안 | 녕 | 히 |  | 가 | 세 | 요 | . |
|---|---|---|---|---|---|---|---|
|  |  |  |  |  |  |  |  |
|  |  |  |  |  |  |  |  |

A 또 만나요.
See you later.

B 또 만나요.
See you later.

| 또 | | 만 | 나 | 요 | . |
|---|---|---|---|---|---|
| | | | | | |
| | | | | | |

A 감사합니다. / 고맙습니다.
Thank you.

B 아니에요.
You're welcome.

| 감 | 사 | 합 | 니 | 다 | . |
|---|---|---|---|---|---|
| | | | | | |
| | | | | | |

| 고 | 맙 | 습 | 니 | 다 | . |
|---|---|---|---|---|---|
| | | | | | |
| | | | | | |

| 아 | 니 | 에 | 요 | . |
|---|---|---|---|---|
| | | | | |
| | | | | |

A 미안합니다. / 죄송합니다.

I'm sorry.

B 괜찮아요.

That's OK.

| 미 | 안 | 합 | 니 | 다 | . |
|---|---|---|---|---|---|
| | | | | | |
| | | | | | |

| 죄 | 송 | 합 | 니 | 다 | . |
|---|---|---|---|---|---|
| | | | | | |
| | | | | | |

| 괜 | 찮 | 아 | 요 | . |
|---|---|---|---|---|
| | | | | |
| | | | | |

A 축하합니다.

Congratulations!

B 감사합니다. / 고맙습니다.

Thank you.

| 축 | 하 | 합 | 니 | 다 | . |
|---|---|---|---|---|---|
| | | | | | |
| | | | | | |

| 감 | 사 | 합 | 니 | 다 | . |
|---|---|---|---|---|---|
| | | | | | |
| | | | | | |

| 고 | 맙 | 습 | 니 | 다 | . |
|---|---|---|---|---|---|
| | | | | | |
| | | | | | |

# 2 자기소개
## Self-Introduction

## 1 이름 말하기 Introducing your Name

Listen to the dialog, and state your own name out loud by using the same sentence structure given in the example.

**Examples**

| | | |
|---|---|---|
| A | 이름이 뭐예요? | What is your name? |
| B | 저는 이름(name) 입니다. | I am ______________ . |
| | 김지수 | Ji-soo Kim |
| | 마이클 | Michael |
| | 앨리스 | alice |
| | 벤자민 | Benjamin |
| | 마리아 | Maria |

## 2 국적 말하기 Introducing your Nationality

Listen to the dialog as you observe the given world map, and state your own nationality out loud by using the same sentence structure given in the example.

**Examples**

A 어느 나라 사람이에요? Where are you from?

B 저는 나라(country) + 사람(person) 입니다. I am from ________.

한국(Korea) Korea

미국(USA) America

| | | | | | | |
|---|---|---|---|---|---|---|
| 1 한국 South Korea | 2 일본 Japan | 3 중국 China | 4 필리핀 The Philippines | 5 인도 India | 6 미국 United States of America | 7 캐나다 Canada |
| 8 영국 United Kingdom | 9 프랑스 France | 10 독일 Germany | 11 러시아 Russia | 12 호주 Australia | 13 뉴질랜드 New Zealand | 14 남아공 South Africa |

Listen to the following words. Then read the words out loud, and write it down.

track 33

| 한 | 국 | | | | |
|---|---|---|---|---|---|
| 한 | 국 | | | | |

| 일 | 본 | | | | |
|---|---|---|---|---|---|
| 일 | 본 | | | | |

| 중 | 국 | | | | |
|---|---|---|---|---|---|
| 중 | 국 | | | | |

| 필 | 리 | 핀 | | | |
|---|---|---|---|---|---|
| 필 | 리 | 핀 | | | |

| 인 | 도 | | | | |
|---|---|---|---|---|---|
| 인 | 도 | | | | |

| 미 | 국 | | | | |
|---|---|---|---|---|---|
| 미 | 국 | | | | |

캐나다
캐나다
영국
영국
프랑스
프랑스
독일
독일
러시아
러시아
호주
호주

뉴질랜드
뉴질랜드
남아공
남아공

## 3 직업 말하기 Introducing your Occupation

Listen to the dialog as you observe the following pictures of jobs, and state your own job out loud by using the same sentence structure given in the example.

**Examples**

A 직업이 뭐예요? What is your job?

B 저는 __직업(job)__ 입니다. I am a ____________.

선생님 teacher

가수 singer

선생님 teacher

학생 student

기자 reporter

회사원 office worker

의사 a doctor

경찰 police

교수 professor

디자이너 designer

가수 singer

운동선수 athlete

요리사 a cook

주부 housewife

Listen to the following words. Then read the words out loud, and write it down.

| | | | | | |
|---|---|---|---|---|---|
| 선 | 생 | 님 | | | |
| 선 | 생 | 님 | | | |
| 학 | 생 | | | | |
| 학 | 생 | | | | |
| 기 | 자 | | | | |
| 기 | 자 | | | | |
| 회 | 사 | 원 | | | |
| 회 | 사 | 원 | | | |
| 의 | 사 | | | | |
| 의 | 사 | | | | |
| 경 | 찰 | | | | |
| 경 | 찰 | | | | |

교 수
교 수
디자이너
디자이너
가 수
가 수
운동선수
운동선수
요 리 사
요 리 사
주 부
주 부

Listen the following dialog, and introduce yourself out loud by using the same sentence structures in the dialog.

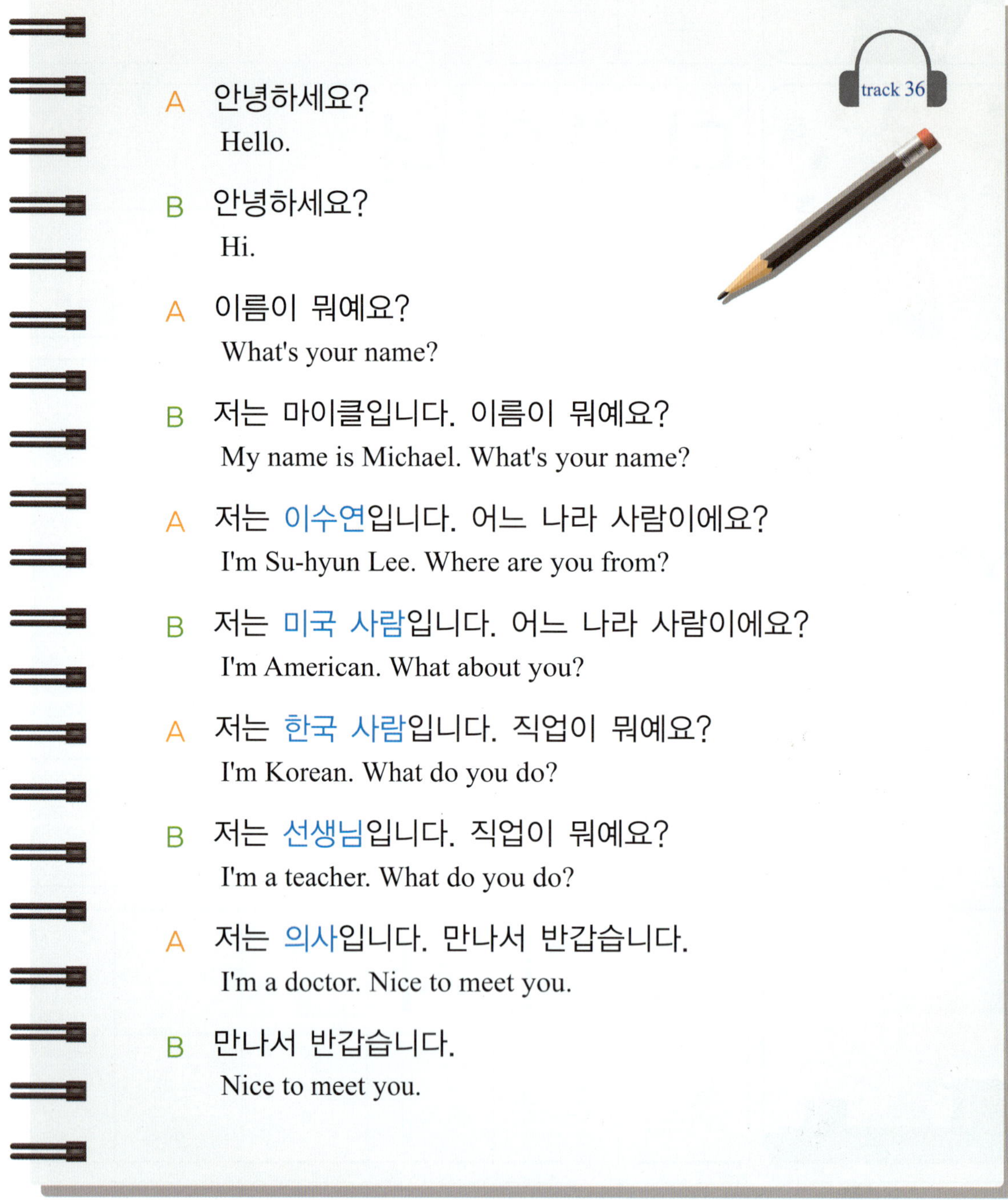


A 안녕하세요?
Hello.

B 안녕하세요?
Hi.

A 이름이 뭐예요?
What's your name?

B 저는 마이클입니다. 이름이 뭐예요?
My name is Michael. What's your name?

A 저는 이수연입니다. 어느 나라 사람이에요?
I'm Su-hyun Lee. Where are you from?

B 저는 미국 사람입니다. 어느 나라 사람이에요?
I'm American. What about you?

A 저는 한국 사람입니다. 직업이 뭐예요?
I'm Korean. What do you do?

B 저는 선생님입니다. 직업이 뭐예요?
I'm a teacher. What do you do?

A 저는 의사입니다. 만나서 반갑습니다.
I'm a doctor. Nice to meet you.

B 만나서 반갑습니다.
Nice to meet you.

# 쇼핑하기 3
## Shopping

## 1 물건 가격 묻고 답하기 Asking for prices of items, and giving responses

### 한자숫자 Sino-Korean Numbers

Sino-Korean numbers such as 1(il), 2(yi), and 3(sam) are used to describe sequences of things. Also, they are used to describe years, months, days, bus numbers, floors of buildings, subway numbers, and phone numbers.

| 1 | 2 | 3 | 4 | 5 |
|---|---|---|---|---|
| 일 | 이 | 삼 | 사 | 오 |
| 6 | 7 | 8 | 9 | 10 |
| 육 | 칠 | 팔 | 구 | 십 |
| 11 | 12 | 13 | 14 | 15 |
| 십일 | 십이 | 십삼 | 십사 | 십오 |
| 16 | 17 | 18 | 19 | 20 |
| 십육 | 십칠 | 십팔 | 십구 | 이십 |
| 30 | 40 | 50 | 60 | 70 |
| 삼십 | 사십 | 오십 | 육십 | 칠십 |
| 80 | 90 | 100 | 1000 | 0 |
| 팔십 | 구십 | 백 | 천 | 영/공 |

Observe the Sino-Korean form of the number given in the example, and re-write all of the following numbers in the chart in their Sino-Korean forms. Then, read the numbers out loud in their Sino-Korean forms.

| 보기 | 210,000 |
| --- | --- |
| | 이십일만 |

Answer page 129

| 21 | 8,540 | 16,700 | 754,321 |
| --- | --- | --- | --- |
| | | | |
| 68 | 4,389 | 74,100 | 987,500 |
| | | | |
| 153 | 12,000 | 257,100 | 1,794,500 |
| | | | |

Listen to the dialog, and state the price of the given items out loud by using the same sentence structures in the dialog.

Let's now play the '3, 6, 9' Game.

**Directions** 3 6 9 Game

Each of the players takes turn around the circle stating Sino-Korean numbers out loud in ascending order, starting from '1' (il). Whenever it is a player's turn to state a number that contains a 3, 6, or 9, the player must clap his/her hands instead of stating the number out loud. For example, the numbers 13, 16, 19, and 30 contain a 3, 6, or 9; hence the player must clap his/her hands instead of stating these numbers out loud. If any player states these numbers, he/she receives a penalty.

## 2 물건 사기 Purchasing Items

### 고유숫자 Pure Korean Number

Pure Korean Numbers are used along with Countable Noun Expressions.
For example, '한 명, 한 개'

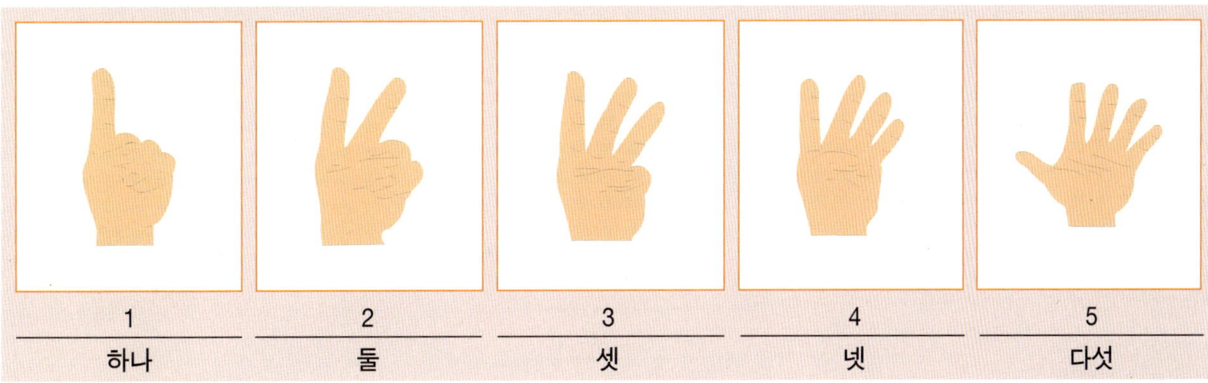

| 1 | 2 | 3 | 4 | 5 |
|---|---|---|---|---|
| 하나 | 둘 | 셋 | 넷 | 다섯 |

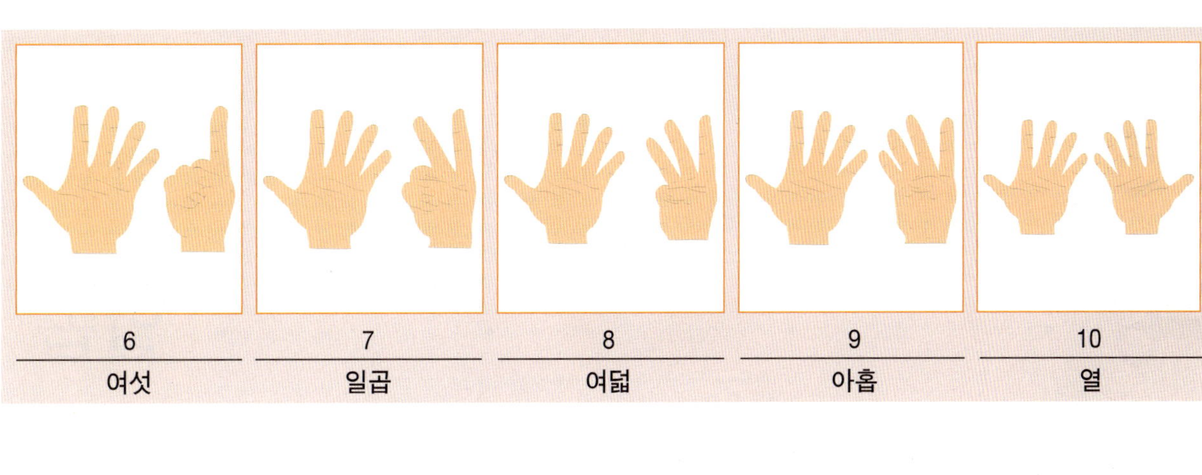

| 6 | 7 | 8 | 9 | 10 |
|---|---|---|---|---|
| 여섯 | 일곱 | 여덟 | 아홉 | 열 |

| 11 | 12 | 13 | 14 | 15 |
|---|---|---|---|---|
| 열하나 | 열둘 | 열셋 | 열넷 | 열다섯 |

| 20 | 30 | 40 | 50 | 60 |
|---|---|---|---|---|
| 스물 | 서른 | 마흔 | 쉰 | 예순 |

| 70 | 80 | 90 | 100 | 0 |
|---|---|---|---|---|
| 일흔 | 여든 | 아흔 | 백 | 영/공 |

Match the following numbers with the correct finger gestures and Pure Korean numbers.

| | |
|---|---|
| 1 | 여섯 |
| 2 | 아홉 |
| 3 | 둘 |
| 4 | 다섯 |
| 5 | 하나 |
| 6 | 일곱 |
| 7 | 셋 |
| 8 | 여덟 |
| 9 | 넷 |
| 10 | 열 |

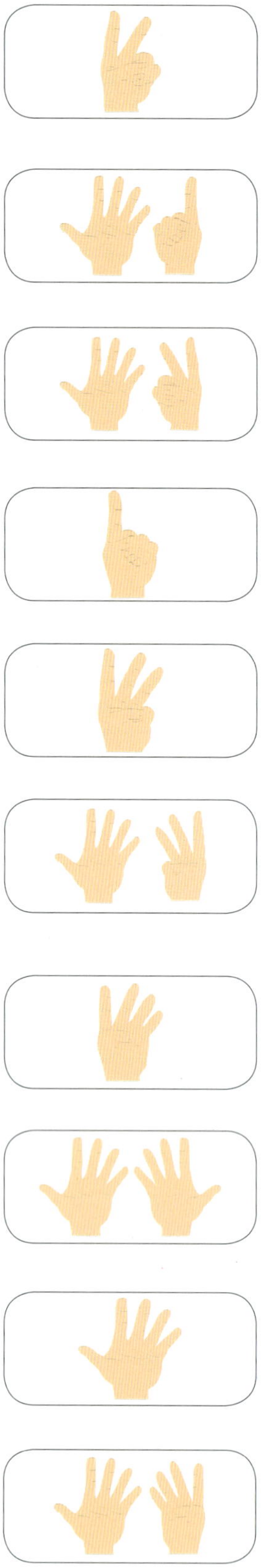

Read the following expressions out loud.

| 숫자 | | | | |
|---|---|---|---|---|
| 1 | *한 개 | 한 명 | 한 잔 | 한 마리 |
| 2 | *두 개 | 두 명 | 두 잔 | 두 마리 |
| 3 | *세 개 | 세 명 | 세 잔 | 세 마리 |
| 4 | *네 개 | 네 명 | 네 잔 | 네 마리 |
| 5 | 다섯 개 | 다섯 명 | 다섯 잔 | 다섯 마리 |
| ⋮ | ⋮ | ⋮ | ⋮ | ⋮ |
| 10 | 열 개 | 열 명 | 열 잔 | 열 마리 |
| ⋮ | ⋮ | ⋮ | ⋮ | ⋮ |
| 20 | *스무 개 | 스무 명 | 스무 잔 | 스무 마리 |

* Pure Korean Numbers such as '하나, 둘, 셋, 넷, and 스물' change into '한, 두, 세, 네, and 스무' when describing Countable Nouns.

Listen to the dialog, and state the price and quantity of the given items out loud by using the same sentence structures in the dialog.

**Examples**

A 우유 있어요? — Is there any milk ?

B 네, 있어요. — Yes, there is.

A 우유 두 개 주세요. — Please give me two milk

B 이천사 백 원입니다. — It is 2,400 won .

# 택시 이용하기 4
## Riding Taxis

## 1 가고 싶은 장소 말하기 Describing Destinations

Listen to the statement as you observe the given pictures of destinations, and state the destinations out loud by using the same sentence structure given in the example.

**Examples**

* 장소(Place) 에 가 주세요. Please go to ___________.

인천공항 Incheon Airport

학교 school

* You can fill in the blank with the name of any place where you want to go.

공항 airport

식당 restaurant

은행 bank

병원 hospital

시장 a market

학교 school

집 a house

교회 church

약국 pharmacy

화장실 restroom

극장 theater

노래방 karaoke room

Listen to the following words. Then read the words out loud, and write it down.

| | | | | | |
|---|---|---|---|---|---|
| 공 | 항 | | | | |
| 공 | 항 | | | | |
| 식 | 당 | | | | |
| 식 | 당 | | | | |
| 은 | 행 | | | | |
| 은 | 행 | | | | |
| 병 | 원 | | | | |
| 병 | 원 | | | | |
| 시 | 장 | | | | |
| 시 | 장 | | | | |
| 학 | 교 | | | | |
| 학 | 교 | | | | |

| 집 | | | | | |
|---|---|---|---|---|---|
| 집 | | | | | |

| 교 | 회 | | | | |
|---|---|---|---|---|---|
| 교 | 회 | | | | |

| 약 | 국 | | | | |
|---|---|---|---|---|---|
| 약 | 국 | | | | |

TOILET

| 화 | 장 | 실 | | | |
|---|---|---|---|---|---|
| 화 | 장 | 실 | | | |

| 극 | 장 | | | | |
|---|---|---|---|---|---|
| 극 | 장 | | | | |

| 노 | 래 | 방 | | | |
|---|---|---|---|---|---|
| 노 | 래 | 방 | | | |

## 2 방향 말하기 Giving Directions

Listen to the dialog as you observe the given pictures of directions, and state the directions out loud by using the same sentence structure given in the example.

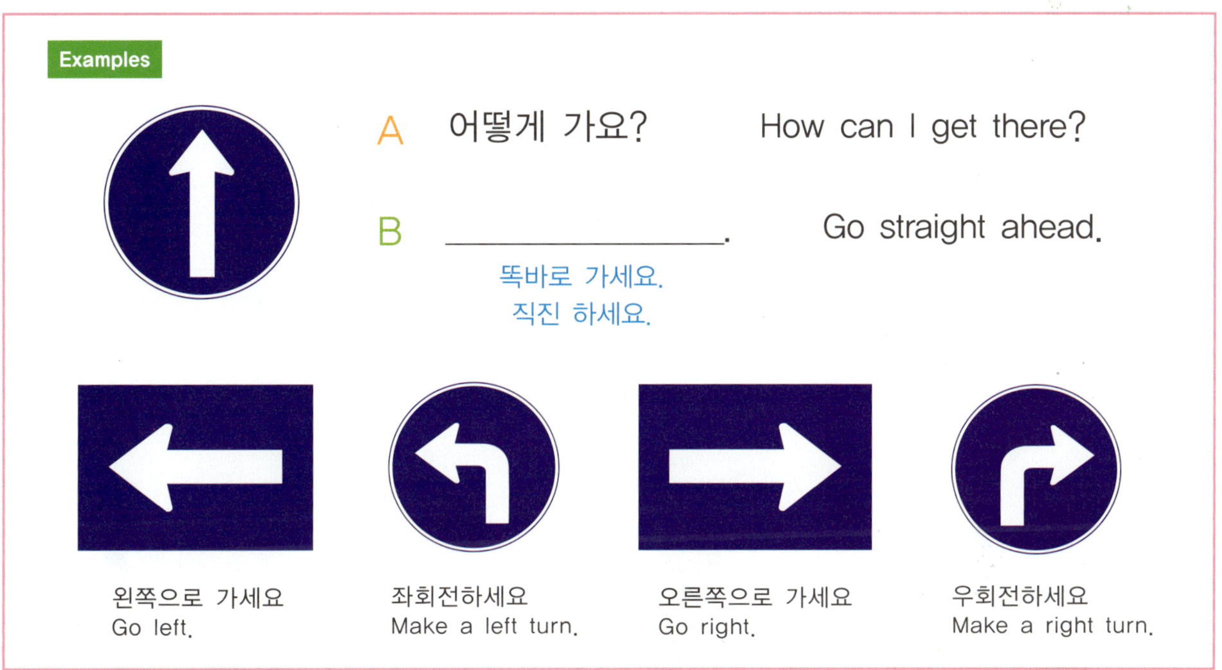


Observe the given picture, and write down the appropriate sentences to give the following three directions as indicated by the arrows.

1 ________________________________________.

2 ________________________________________.

3 ________________________________________.

## 3 위치 말하기 Describing Locations

Listen to the dialog as you observe the given pictures of locations, and state the locations out loud by using the same sentence structures in the dialog.

**Examples**

A ________ 어디에 있어요? Where is ________ ?

학교 / 은행 — school / bank

B *N(place) location 에 있어요. It is located ____________ .

병원 앞 / 시장 옆 — in front of hospital / next to the market

* N에 있어요 : location, 'to be (located in a place)' or 'to stay'

위 top

아래 bottom

앞 front

뒤 back

사이 between

안 inside

밖 outside

왼쪽 left

오른쪽 right

Listen to the following words. Then read the words out loud, and write it down.

| 위 | | | | | |
|---|---|---|---|---|---|
| 위 | | | | | |

| 아 | 래 | | | | |
|---|---|---|---|---|---|
| 아 | 래 | | | | |

| 앞 | | | | | |
|---|---|---|---|---|---|
| 앞 | | | | | |

| 뒤 | | | | | |
|---|---|---|---|---|---|
| 뒤 | | | | | |

| 사 | 이 | | | | |
|---|---|---|---|---|---|
| 사 | 이 | | | | |

| 안 | | | | | |
|---|---|---|---|---|---|
| 안 | | | | | |

| 밖 | | | | | |
|---|---|---|---|---|---|
| 밖 | | | | | |

| 왼 | 쪽 | | | | |
|---|---|---|---|---|---|
| 왼 | 쪽 | | | | |

| 오 | 른 | 쪽 | | | |
|---|---|---|---|---|---|
| 오 | 른 | 쪽 | | | |

Unit Ⅳ

# 부록 Appendix

단어 색인 Vocabulary Index

정답 Answer

단어 카드 Picture Cards

# 단어 색인 Vocabulary Index

# 단어 색인 Vocabulary Index

## Unit Ⅱ 한글

### Chapter1. 기본모음

page 23

page 23

# 정답 Answer

## Chapter2 자음

page 56

## Chapter3 복합모음

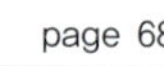
page 68

page 69

## Chapter4 받침

page 68

| | | | | | | | |
|---|---|---|---|---|---|---|---|
| 나 | 다 | 섯 | 의 | 살 | 한 | 국 | 던 |
| 얼 | 던 | 고 | 향 | 은 | 국 | 꽃 | 피 |
| 굴 | 산 | 가 | 족 | 골 | 어 | 복 | 숭 |
| 아 | 꽃 | 살 | 구 | 꽃 | 아 | 기 | 진 |
| 가 | 달 | 엄 | 울 | 여 | 긋 | 불 | 자 |
| 방 | 긋 | 마 | 대 | 덟 | 궐 | 차 | 전 |
| 리 | 부 | 흰 | 동 | 네 | 그 | 속 | 거 |
| 에 | 엌 | 서 | 많 | 놀 | 던 | 때 | 가 |
| 그 | 립 | 습 | 다 | 니 | 선 | 생 | 님 |
| 다 | 장 | 미 | 꽃 | 동 | 네 | 새 | 동 |
| 네 | 나 | 의 | 옛 | 순 | 가 | 락 | 고 |
| 향 | 태 | 극 | 기 | 파 | 란 | 들 | 남 |

## Unit Ⅲ 서바이벌 한국어

### Chapter3 쇼핑

page 109

| 21 | 8,540 | 16,700 | 754,321 |
|---|---|---|---|
| 이십일 | 팔천오백사십 | 만육천칠백 | 칠십오만사천삼백이십일 |
| 68 | 4,389 | 74,100 | 987,500 |
| 육십팔 | 사천삼백팔십구 | 칠만사천백 | 구십팔만칠천오백 |
| 153 | 12,000 | 257,100 | 1,794,500 |
| 백오십삼 | 사천삼백팔십구 | 칠만사천백 | 구십팔만칠천오백 |

# 단어 카드

Picture Cards

· Cut the cards out along the dotted line, and carry them around to use their contents accordingly.

- 단어 카드 Common Vocabulary Words
- 인사말 카드 Greetings
- 국가 카드 Nationalities
- 직업 카드 Occupations
- 장소 카드 Destinations
- 방향과 위치 카드 Directions and Locations

MILK

| | |
|---|---|
| 이 | 오 |
| 아우 | 아이 |
| 우유 | 오이 |
| 야구 | 여우 |

35
8years
11
Happy

Here

| | |
|---|---|
| 나이 | 고기 |
| 구두 | 누나 |
| 오리 | 다리 |
| 여기 | 가구 |

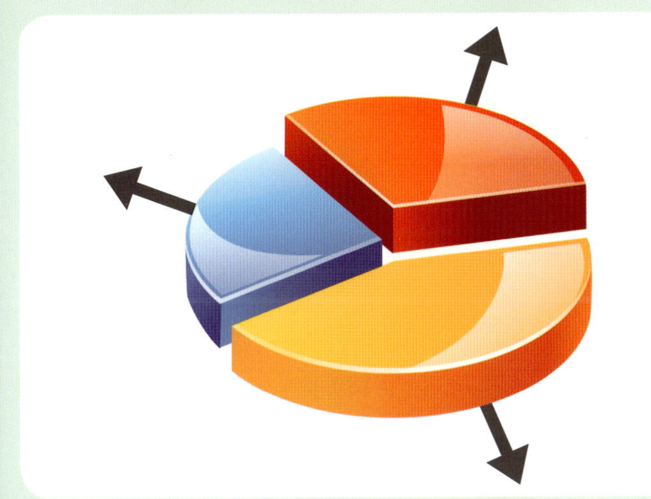

Here
37

soap

| | |
|---|---|
| 아니요 | 너 |
| 오다 | 나누다 |
| 나무 | 기러기 |
| 비누 | 머리 |

School Bus

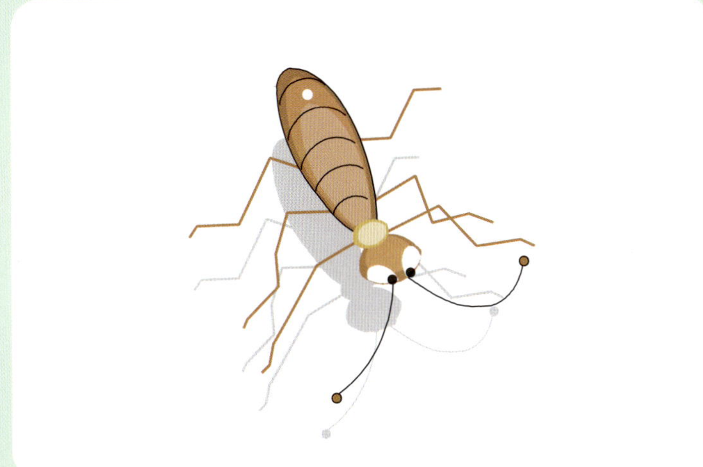

서다

나비

모자

버스

모기

거미

바나나

바구니

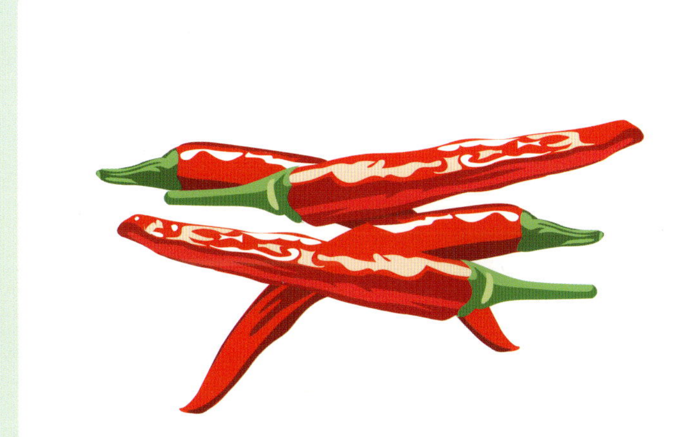

| | |
|---|---|
| 소리 | 사다리 |
| 고추 | 여자 |
| 기차 | 치마 |
| 크다 | 키 |

RABBIT
ANGEL

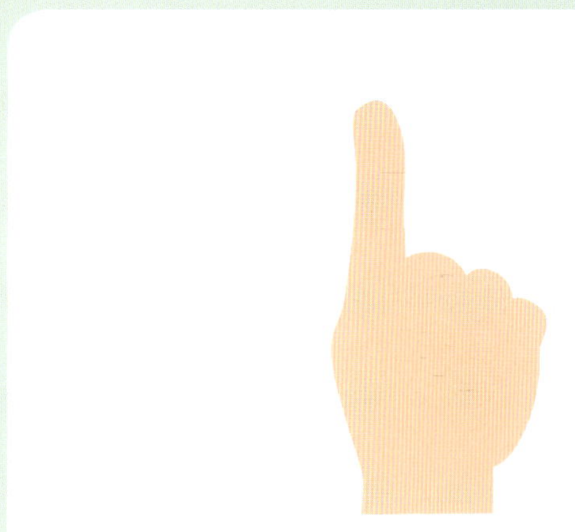

커피

코트

투수

타다

아프다

티셔츠

하나

포도

CITYHALL
NARU SUBWAY

7

₩ 50,000,000

까치

지하

따다

꼬리

아빠

로또

비싸다

뽀뽀

Vintage Flower

SALT

| | |
|---|---|
| 짜다 | 쓰다 |
| 머리띠 | 코끼리 |
| 뿌리 | 따르다 |
| 싸우다 | 바쁘다 |

12
1
2
3
4
5
6
7
8
9
10
11

가짜

아가씨

그네

찌르다

애기

개미

사과

시계

| | |
|---|---|
| 교회 | 돼지 |
| 세다 | 세수 |
| 해바라기 | 무지개 |
| 회사 | 화가 |

RUN

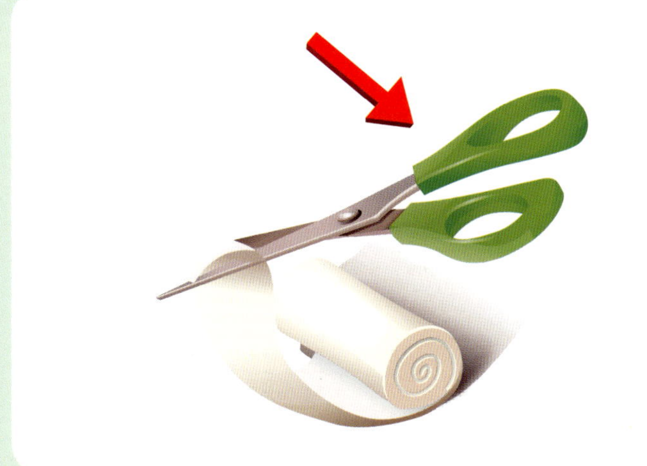

샤워

열쇠

쥐

뛰다

주사위

가위

스웨터

의사

KOREA
KOREA
KOREA

Toothpaste

BREAD

| | |
|---|---|
| 가족 | 맥주 |
| 학교 | 치약 |
| 깎다 | 부엌 |
| 산 | 낚시 |

1000

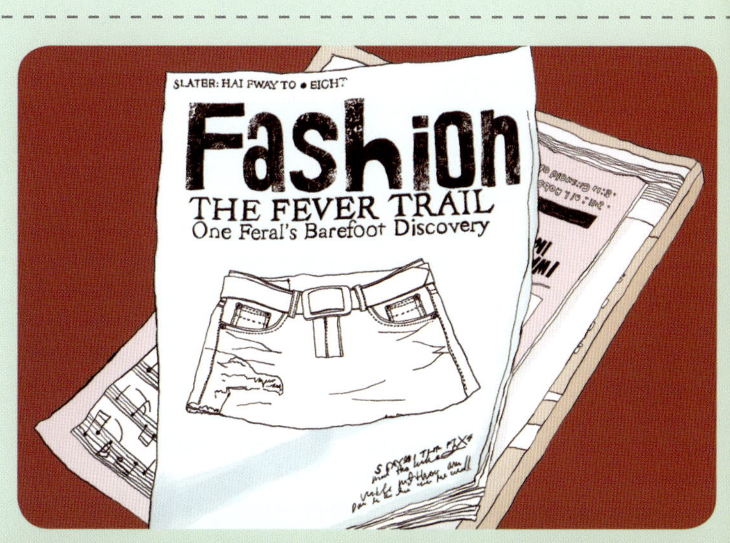
SLATER: HAI FWAY TO • EIGHT
Fashion
THE FEVER TRAIL
One Feral's Barefoot Discovery

| | |
|---|---|
| 말 | 돈 |
| 얼굴 | 연필 |
| 인삼 | 남자 |
| 잡지 | 집 |

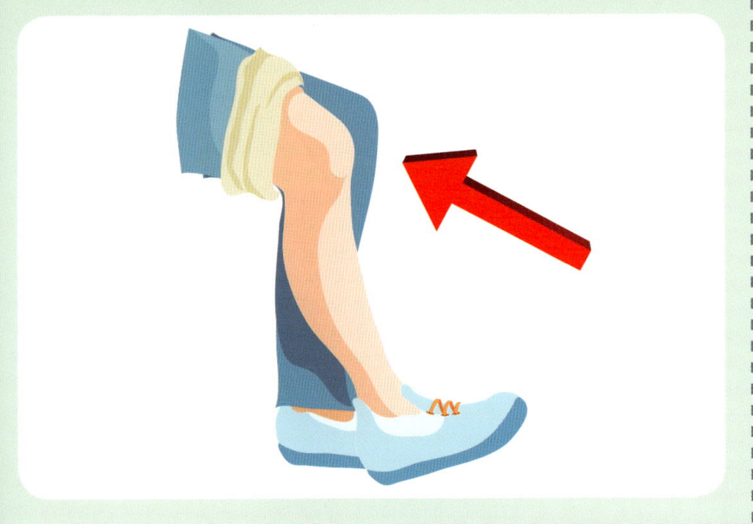

| 지갑 | 무릎 |
| --- | --- |
| 앞 | 가방 |
| 선생님 | 학생 |
| 듣다 | 걷다 |

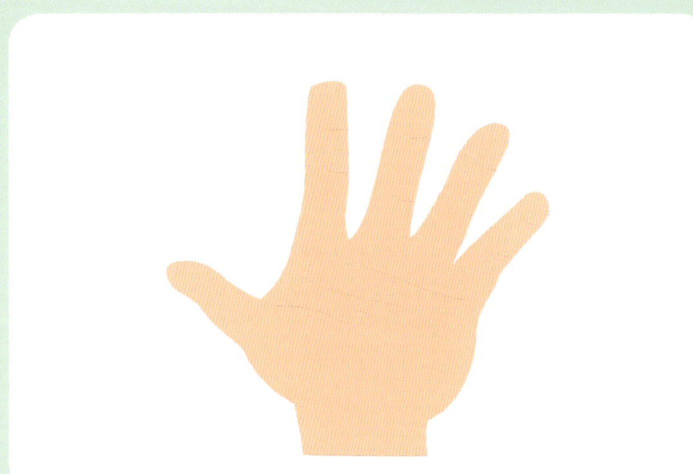

| | |
|---|---|
| 돋보기 | 숟가락 |
| 다섯 | 밭 |
| 버섯 | 칫솔 |
| 낮 | 젓가락 |

흥

8

햇빛

낮잠

히읗

꽃

닭

여덟

앉다

읽다

10000
10000
10000

넓다

많다

값

만나서 반갑습니다.

안녕하세요?

안녕히 가세요.
안녕히 가세요.

안녕히 가세요.
안녕히 계세요.

갑사합니다.
고맙습니다.
아니예요.

또 만나요.
또 만나요.

축하합니다.
감사합니다.
고맙습니다.

미안합니다.
죄송합니다.
괜찮아요.

일본

한국

필리핀

중국

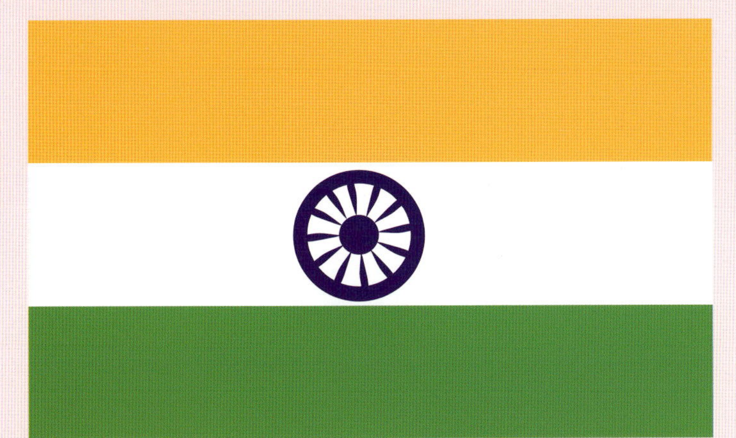

미국

인도

영국

캐나다

독일

프랑스

호주

러시아

| | |
|---|---|
| 남아공 | 뉴질랜드 |
| 학생 | 선생님 |
| 회사원 | 기자 |
| 경찰 | 의사 |

디자이너

교수

운동선수

가수

주부

요리사

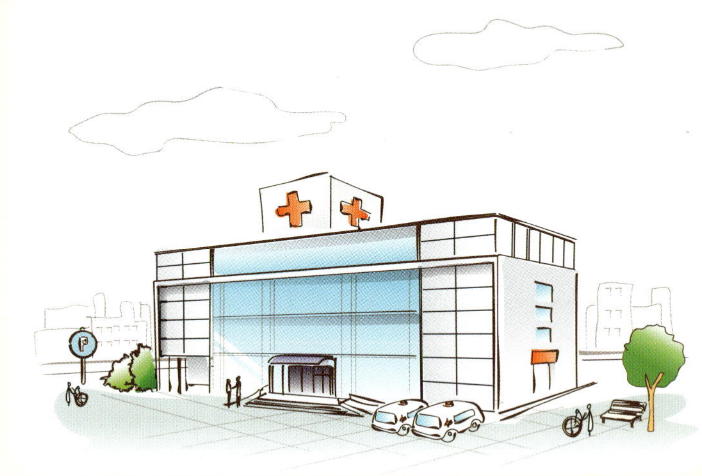

식당

공항

병원

은행

학교

시장

교회

집

TOILET

URGENT
FRAGILE

URGENT
FRAGILE

URGENT
FRAGILE

URGENT
FRAGILE

| | |
|---|---|
| 화장실 | 약국 |
| 노래방 | 극장 |
| 아래 | 위 |
| 뒤 | 앞 |

안

사이

왼쪽

밖

오른쪽